Feelings

Feelings

Poetry by Bruce B. Wilmer

Published and printed by:
Wilmer Graphics, Inc.
P. O. Box 140, Huntington, NY 11743

With special thanks to all the staff at Wilmer Graphics who have contributed their skills and advice to the printing and manufacture of this book.

Manufactured in the United States of America

First printing: February, 1987

2 3 4 5 6 7 8 9 10 — 91 90 89 88 87

ISBN: 0-9615967-0-8

For Syd...

My wife, my love, my dearest friend

INTRODUCTION

My writing began as an antidote to an unexpected three year Army tour from 1968-71, which interrupted law school. Writing turned from avocation to vocation in 1976 when my compulsion to write finally displaced practicality entirely. My wife indulged my abandonment of conventional employment by dropping her teaching career and joining with me in a business venture appropriately known as Wilmer Graphics. Poetry as a business is difficult to explain to those who see it as a break from normal middle class ranks. My family's artistic and creative background, however, made this seemingly imprudent leap easy for me to accomplish. My life was never "right" until I turned this corner. Turning it was my key to happiness; I have never looked back with regret. Security can be elusive, and life isn't always easy; but if you're in phase with your inner self, it certainly helps.

Many of the poems in FEELINGS have appeared on greeting cards and graphic products under my LIGHT LINES trademark. This creative format places many into the category of communicative or purposeful poetry. They are simple and direct, hopefully not greeting card simplistic. Some of my poems are introspective; while some attempt to understand and empathize with the feelings and experiences of others. They are generally positive in intent, seeking to promote communication, understanding, growth. They verbalize warmth and affection. They often muse at and enthuse over life's mysteries. Without trying to contribute to life's puzzles, they seek to address them. They strive for musicality through the use of rhyme, meter, flow.

After ten years, I must admit that the business side of Wilmer Graphics is often all-consuming; and writing is still almost an avocation, a thing I do for the love of it in spare moments snatched as an antidote to life's full routine. Fortunately, this routine is largely an expression of my creative yearnings and my avocation is not so much an escape as a positive outlet for my perpetually reactive personality.

My satisfaction is greatest when a poem of mine aids communication, promotes positive thoughts, reduces isolation, reinforces love and friendship, captures the emotions, liberates the spirit. Despite my practical business side, my idealism still craves this room to operate.

The consummate result for me as a writer was obtained with a poem in this volume entitled Mother Rose, written for my mother when her strength was ebbing after a disabling stroke. Presented to her on her last Valentine's Day when normal communication was nearly impossible, and read to her by my father, the only reply she was capable of proved to be more than enough. Her quiet tears welded in my soul forever the supreme power of a poetic image. This poignant response will remain always as my highest measure of poetic achievement and a true model of what I want to accomplish with art and life.

—Bruce B. Wilmer

CONTENTS

A FRIEND   1
I'M THINKING OF YOU   2
I'LL BE THERE   3
YOU ARE MY FRIEND   4
I'M GLAD THERE'S YOU   5
FRIENDSHIP   7
THANK YOU FOR BEING YOU   8
YOU'RE LIKE FAMILY TO ME   9
YOU MADE MY DAY   10
YOU'RE SPECIAL TO ME   11
WHAT IS A FRIEND?   12
I UNDERSTAND   13
WE'VE SHARED A LOT   14
I THINK ABOUT YOU OFTEN   16
FRIENDS FOREVER   17
PORTRAIT OF A FRIEND   18
MY BEST FRIEND   19
GOODBYE, MY FRIEND   21
OUR GROUP   22
HOW ARE YOU DOING?   23
IT'S HARD TO BE OBJECTIVE   24
THANK YOU FOR CARING   25
DEAR MOM   27
YOU TOOK THE TIME   28
YOU'VE GIVEN SO MUCH   29
DEAR DAD   30
THANK YOU FOR BEING MY PARENT   31
I'M YOUR PARENT, I'M YOUR FRIEND   32
YOU'RE MY PARENT, YOU'RE MY FRIEND   33
THANK YOU FOR BELIEVING IN ME   34
BELIEVE IN YOURSELF   36
FOLLOW YOUR HEART   37
YOU'LL FIND THE ANSWER   38
BE DIFFERENT, BUT DON'T BE THE SAME   40
THE ART OF LIVING   41
YOU ARE MY FAMILY   43

WILDFLOWER   44
OUR LIVES TOUCHED   46
MY FRIEND, MY LOVER   47
SHARE WITH ME   48
I ENJOY BEING WITH YOU   49
IF I SEEM INDEPENDENT   51
TWO FREE   52
YOU'RE MORE THAN A FRIEND   53
I LOVE YOUR MYSTERY   54
LET'S TAKE OUR TIME   56
I'LL WAIT FOR YOU   57
COME SHARE MY LIFE   59
LEND ME LOVE   60
TOGETHER   61
WHEN WE ARE APART   62
I MISS YOU   64
YOU FILL MY THOUGHTS   65
YOU ARE ON MY MIND   67
I NEED YOU   68
YOU'RE MY FANTASY   69
LOVE IS A RAINBOW   70
WITH YOU, I'M ME   72
WE NEED EACH OTHER   73
SOMETHING HAPPENED IN MY HEART   75
I'M CRAZY OVER YOU   76
YOU TURN ME ON   77
YOU ARE MY POETRY   79
HONEYSUCKLE   80
THROUGH OUR EYES   81
OUR UNIVERSE   82
YOU ARE MY INSPIRATION   83
OUR RELATIONSHIP IS SPECIAL   84
THE PERFECT TWO   86
I LOVE YOU   87
YOU AND I   89
I'M FEELING CLOSE TO YOU   90
FOR MY LOVE   91

LOVE IS ALWAYS THERE   93
I BELIEVE IN US   94
LOVE IS…   95
ALL I WANT IS YOU   96
THE ONE I LOVE   98
MARRIAGE OF TWO HEARTS   99
MY WIFE, MY LOVE   100
WE HAVE IT ALL   101
OUR LOVE   103
I'M SECURE IN YOU   104
YOU ARE MY STAR   105
YOU'RE PERFECT IN MY EYES   106
A TIME FOR US   108
I WANT YOU   109
HAPPY BIRTHDAY, SWEETHEART   110
THAT ENERGY CALLED LOVE   111
STAY CLOSE TO ME   112
I LOVE YOU MORE EACH DAY   114
PLEASE SAVE SOME TIME FOR ME   115
I NEED A HUG   116
I'M SENSITIVE TO YOU   118
LOVE MAKES IT WORK   119
WE'RE A COUPLE OF NUTS   121
LET'S RELAX   122
WE'RE UNDER A LOT OF STRESS   123
I'M FEELING A LITTLE LONELY   124
LOVE IS A WORD   126
LET'S MAKE IT WORK   127
I NEED TIME TO THINK   128
WE NEED TO TALK   129
I NEED TO TALK IT OUT   130
IT'S TIME TO OPEN UP   131
LET ME UNDERSTAND YOU   133
I TRUSTED YOU   134
YOU LET YOUR REAL SELF SHOW   135
NOBODY IS PERFECT   136
PLEASE BE PATIENT WITH ME   137

I ACTED WITHOUT THINKING   138
I'M SORRY   139
DON'T PLACE ME ON A PEDESTAL   140
LET'S COMMUNICATE   142
A TIME FOR UNDERSTANDING   143
LET'S FORGIVE AND FORGET   144
LET'S PUT IT BEHIND US   145
CAN'T WE JUST BE FRIENDS   147
LET'S STILL BE FRIENDS   148
LET'S BE GRACIOUS IN PARTING   149
LOVE WAS UNKIND TO YOU   150
OUR FAMILY HAS CHANGED   151
I WANT YOU BACK   152
I CARE FOR YOU   153
LET'S BLAME IT ON THE PAST   154
I AM MAD AT NOTHING   155
I'M ONLY HUMAN   156
I NEED SOME TIME FOR MYSELF   157
THINGS WILL GET BETTER   158
THAT STRENGTH FROM WITHIN   160
LIFE ISN'T ALWAYS EASY   161
IT'S HOW YOU COPE   163
IF YOU HAVE A PROBLEM   164
LET'S MAKE THE MOST OF LIFE   165
I BELIEVE IN YOU   166
YOU CAN MAKE A DIFFERENCE   167
FOLLOW YOUR DREAMS   168
IF YOU NEVER TRY   170
TAKE CHARGE OF YOUR LIFE   171
THE GOAL   172
I'M PROUD OF YOU   174
THE GIFT NOT TAKEN   176
WHAT IS SUCCESS?   177
HAPPINESS   179
FISHERMAN'S LAW   180
SUCCESS   181
NEW BEGINNINGS   182

CREATIVITY IS... 185
THE CREATIVE PERSON 186
✳ THE GIFT OF TEACHING 187
IDENTITY PRAYER 188
BUMBLEBEE 190
HOLY WAR 191
LUMINESCENCE 192
NATURE'S FALL 193
DON'T START 194
TO OUR HEALTH 195
PORTRAIT OF A GREEN THUMB 196
DEWDROP 197
CLOSE TO LIFE 199
YOUTH 200
CHALLENGER 201
WHEN TIME STANDS STILL 202
A SPACE IN TIME 204
TEARS OF SPRING 205
TAKE A MINUTE 207
SURVIVOR 208
MIND AND SPIRIT 210
I'M ALONE WITH MYSELF 211
MELANCHOLY MOMENTS 212
SOJOURN WITH SLEEP 213
THE SEASON OF OUR SORROW 214
MOTHER ROSE 215
REMEMBER WITH THE HEART 216
LITTLE BIRD 218
MY PRAYER 219
THE WINDOW 220
HOME IS IN THE HEART 222
TOM 224
A BABY'S SMILE 228
A CHILD'S WORLD 230
TODAY'S CHILD 233
A SISTER IS FOREVER 234
LITTLE GIRL 237

Poetry is a contagious tear.

A FRIEND

A friend's an attitude within you,
A talk you always can continue,
A feeling you have known a while,
A thought that sparks an inner smile.

A friend's a person you hold dear,
Who ventures far, yet stays quite near,
Whose presence sets the spirit free,
Who brings out candor, honesty.

A friend shares all your joys and tears,
Feels triumph with you, knows your fears,
Accepts your strengths and weakness, too,
Won't let small things dull friendship's hue.

A friend will walk life's miles with you
And nourish values sound and true.
Though paths may sometimes drift apart,
True friendship never leaves the heart.

I'M THINKING OF YOU

My mind is moving silently,
   Fond memories selecting.
I linger long with thoughts of you,
   Remembering, reflecting.

In moments when the mind is free
   It makes impromptu choices;
And as it drifts from thought to thought
   It summons certain voices.

When time permits my thoughts to drift
   Through tides of fond recall,
I recreate the times we've shared,
   Those moments large and small.

And when I'm roused from reverie,
   An inner feeling yearns
For many more such moments
   When the thought of you returns.

I'LL BE THERE

If ever there's a moment
   When you need a friend to listen,
If ever someone can reach out
   To dry the tears that glisten,
           I'll be there.

If ever you have special needs
   And hope someone will see them,
If ever you have secrets
   And would like a friend to free them,
           I'll be there.

If you just need encouragement
   To help you on the way,
If you just need a cheerful voice
   To pull you through the day,
           I'll be there.

If you need one who cares a lot
   And thinks about you often,
If you need one who shares your hopes—
   Your worries strives to soften,
           I'll be there.

If you would like to be yourself
   With someone who respects you,
If you need one who understands
   How all of life affects you,
           I'll be there.

YOU ARE MY FRIEND

You are my friend—
　　You stir me inside
To let you in closer,
　　To share, to confide.

You are a message
　　I give to my heart.
It says that in spirit
　　We never will part.

You are a feeling
　　That lives in my mind
And wants to explore
　　All the meanings we find.

You are a part of me;
　　We are the same
In granting each other
　　Affectionate fame.

Ours is a story
　　That hasn't an end.
We've written the chapters
　　On being a friend.

I'M GLAD THERE'S YOU

When life around us bubbles
    In a most chaotic brew,
I can say in words right from the heart
    I'm very glad there's you.

For in this wacky world of ours
    Through which we all are drifting,
Your influence is positive;
    Your manner is uplifting.

You add to life in your own way;
    You give when others borrow;
You chase away the clouds
    And then predict a bright tomorrow.

Your outlook is refreshing;
    Life for you is never stale.
You bring enthusiasm
    To each moment without fail.

Your energy gives life a boost—
    Your cheerful manner, too.
You give that rarest gift, yourself—
    I'm very glad there's you.

FRIENDSHIP

Friendship is a warming wind
   That gently heralds spring.
It speaks of new beginnings
   And all life has to bring.

Friendship is the sun-filled days
   That summer has to share,
With openness and freedom
   And learning how to care.

Friendship is the ripened fruit
   That comes as autumn's gift.
It nourishes and keeps us strong
   And gives our hearts a lift.

Friendship is the lasting roots
   That thrive through winter snows
And grow still deeper through the trials
   Only friendship knows.

Friendship is a vital force
   That grows for many reasons
And like the tallest, strongest tree
   Endures throughout the seasons.

THANK YOU FOR BEING YOU

There are artificial people
    Living artificial ways
With many artificial things
    To occupy their days.

That's why it's so refreshing
    To be with you a while
And find someone who's natural
    In manner and in style.

A person who is genuine
    Is someone hard to find.
Your graciousness and honesty
    Are admirably combined.

You're truly an exception;
    Your qualities are rare.
When winds of life distract me,
    You're a breath of pure fresh air.

YOU'RE LIKE FAMILY TO ME

Because you've been so very close
And friendly all these years
And since you've been beside me
Through the joys and through the tears,
You're like family to me.

Because you're someone I can count on
When I'm feeling down
And you're the person who can still
Erase a stubborn frown,
You're like family to me.

Because there's hardly anything
I can't discuss with you
And you accept me as I am
And hear my point of view,
You're like family to me.

Because I share concern for you
As you're concerned for me,
And friendship still can flourish
Even when we disagree,
You're like family to me.

And since there's nothing deeper
Than the feelings that we share
And our sincere relationship
Is filled with loving care,
You're like family to me.

YOU MADE MY DAY

I just want you to know that
   In a most appealing way
You lifted up my spirits—
   Yes, you really made my day.

You channeled all my thinking
   In a positive direction.
You gave a rather normal day
   A look of near perfection.

You made the day seem special—
   It's a pleasure to admit it.
Your kindly deed struck me just right;
   And I'm so glad you did it.

Your timely gesture made me feel
   Much better all around.
Your impact on this day of mine
   Was lasting and profound.

YOU'RE SPECIAL TO ME

You're special to me—
You're someone I trust.
I treasure the topics
That we have discussed.

I'm thankful for times
You have summoned a smile.
I'm grateful our paths
Have converged for a while.

I'm pleased by each confidence
You have displayed.
I cherish those moments
You've sought to persuade.

I'm touched by the gestures
Of kindness you've shown.
I've noticed how fast
All our hours have flown.

I'm feeling the force
Of a friendship that's true.
I'm fortunate knowing
A person like you.

WHAT IS A FRIEND?

A friend is a person
  Whose name comes to mind
When the meaning of friendship
  You're trying to find.

A friend is the one who
  Deserves recognition
For giving to friendship
  Its best definition.

I UNDERSTAND

Life's events don't always happen
Just as they are planned.
For you this is a trying time—
I fully understand.

Moments like the present
Tend to upset and confuse.
I'll try to give you my support
In any path you choose.

I'll listen always with my heart;
I'll do what I can do.
I'll hope for better things to come;
My thoughts remain with you.

You know your situation—
You're alert to life's demands.
But don't forget that I am here—
I'm one who understands.

WE'VE SHARED A LOT

We've shared a lot together;
  We've walked a common road.
In many ways these moments form
  A special episode.

I can't foresee the future
  Or know how our lives will blend,
But more and more I know that I
  Have found a lasting friend.

It's something rare to find someone
  Whose thought inspires a smile,
Who's shared life's joys and disappointments,
  Traced a common mile.

But I can say with certainty
  That something from inside
Keeps telling me I'm glad you've been
  Companion for the ride.

I THINK ABOUT YOU OFTEN

I think about you often—
  I play a game with time.
I move away the moments lost—
  Time's obstacles I climb.

I minimize the distances
  That separate our lives.
I know that when we're close enough
  Communication thrives.

I conjure up a conversation,
  Improvise your part.
For images and memories
  I delve into my heart.

But when I must conclude the game,
  The meaning lingers true:
Such memories can hardly be
  A substitute for you.

FRIENDS FOREVER

We're joined in a friendship
   That time cannot sever.
With bonds we have built
   We'll remain friends forever.

We're welded in spirit,
   Attached by our hearts.
We're fused by the feeling
   That friendship imparts.

We're tied by emotions,
   Connected by dreams,
Reinforced by our hopes,
   Unified by extremes.

No longer a function
   Of time or of space,
Our love is a substance
   That life won't replace.

No matter how distant,
   We'll always endeavor
To sense the full meaning
   Of friendship forever.

PORTRAIT OF A FRIEND

I gave to you my portrait,
  As friends will often do.
I sketched it rather hastily,
  Left details strong but few.

I gave to you another likeness
  Drawn in colors fine.
The picture was a truer one
  With subtle shade and line.

I gave to you a photograph
  With details sharp and clear,
A natural and candid me
  To share with someone dear.

I gave to you my inner thoughts
  In phrases from the heart;
And in the trust these words revealed
  Was friendship's highest art.

MY BEST FRIEND

You're a friend who passes
    Every warm and heartfelt test
For being there and being true
    And being very best.

You're the one who hears my thoughts
    And understands my thinking.
You're the one who senses first
    When attitudes are sinking.

You know all the strengths
    And all the weaknesses of me.
You know when I need support
    And when to disagree.

You and I confide and share
    The secrets of the soul.
You know when a friend should help
    Or gently yield control.

You are where the heart finds comfort,
    Where the mind is free.
You are more than just a friend;
    You're more than company.

You are where the spirit rests,
    Where tensions disappear.
You are where I find myself—
    When life is hard, you're near.

GOODBYE, MY FRIEND

Goodbye, my friend—
   Goodbye 'til then.
Farewell until
   We meet again.
It may be soon,
   It may be late.
For us it's always
   Worth the wait.

I'll miss our private
   Conversations,
Quiet thoughts and
   Inspirations,
All the times
   We laughed and cried,
All the warmth
   We felt inside.

Let's keep in touch
   In our own way.
Let's share our dreams
   Another day.
Let's never lose
   The things we've shared.
Let's part as friends
   Who've loved and cared.

OUR GROUP

Our group is not the plain variety—
  It's a little-bit-insane society.
It has its scholars, kooks and clowns,
  Its schizophrenic ups and downs,
Its days of work and righteous piety,
  Its days of total insobriety.
It has its weirdos and its straights,
  Its swinging singles with their dates,
Its loyal marrieds so devoted,
  Its members skinny—others bloated.
It has its geniuses and bores,
  Its petty tiffs and civil wars,
Its days of buoyant jubilation,
  Its moments of acute frustration.
It has its faces bright and sunny
  And others who complain of money.
It has its listeners and its talkers,
  Its activists, its chronic balkers,
Its fitness freaks and sugar junkies,
  Workaholics, mental flunkies.
It has its drinkers with their booze,
  Its Pollyannas with good news,
Its leaders with their organizing,
  Its followers all eulogizing,
Its nonconformists nonconforming,
  Its rumor mongers misinforming,
Its malcontents with all their raving,
  Its married members misbehaving,
Its moments crude and moments formal,
  Its members who are oddly normal.
We are a group and none should doubt it,
  Since where would we all be without it.

HOW ARE YOU DOING?

How are you doing?
How are you faring?
You flashed through my mind
In a moment of caring.

How often your image
Has entered my thinking—
A friendly distraction,
A brief mental linking.

This moment's concern,
This fleeting sensation,
Awakens the memory,
Affects concentration.

Then life's full routine
Interrupts and intrudes,
Dissolving completely
These gentlest moods.

Since life goes ahead
At a feverish pace,
I just want to quickly
And fondly touch base.

IT'S HARD TO BE OBJECTIVE

I'd like to be objective,
    Give opinions that are sound.
I'd like to have a balanced view,
    Let common sense abound.

But I am just a bit too close—
    I have a point of view.
I'm not convinced that I can sort
    The biased from the true.

I know my limitations
    As I struggle to be fair.
I have some deeper feelings
    That I cannot help but share.

I cannot guarantee
    I'll be impartial to the end.
I'll offer quite sincerely
    The opinions of a friend.

THANK YOU FOR CARING

When someone takes the time to listen,
    When someone reaches out,
When someone does a thoughtful thing
    That makes you warm throughout,

When someone lends a helping hand,
    Finds ways in which to share,
When someone makes you feel secure
    By always being there,

When someone senses there are times
    When you have special needs,
When someone gives you inner strength
    Through words as well as deeds,

When someone seems to take an interest
    In just how you're faring,
It's time to tell that special someone—
    Thanks so much for caring!

DEAR MOM

I want to say so many things;
    I don't know how to start.
I want to capture and describe
    The feelings of my heart.

But words are so inadequate
    To tell you how I feel
That scarcely any thing I say
    Will my true thoughts reveal.

Just let it now suffice to say
    That deep inside I know
My love for you is something
    That I never will outgrow.

Your many special traits will always
    In my heart combine
In such a way that you alone
    A perfect mom define.

Your warmth and caring are the traits
    That I am proudest of.
My future's brighter through
    The fine example of your love.

YOU TOOK THE TIME

You sensed in me a moment
    Of complete, compelling need.
You ventured in when others
    Wouldn't dare to intercede.

You listened and you talked to me,
    Thus drawing spirits close;
My problems and concerns
    You let me share in ample dose.

Your sensitive response to me
    When my true feelings beckoned
Was fully demonstrated
    When you placed your own cares second.

You let me into your life
    At a moment that was prime.
I needed you and you replied
    By giving me the time.

YOU'VE GIVEN SO MUCH

A person is most vulnerable
    When someone else is giving,
And taking very often is
    The hardest part of living.

You sensed a moment of true need
    When I was down and shaken;
You've given all that you could give,
    But then you haven't taken.

To give and then seek no return,
    Just satisfied with sharing,
Is a truly noble act—
    The highest form of caring.

It's possible to give and then
    Exact a moral price;
But you instead in your unselfish
    Way have been so nice.

Assistance from another
    Isn't easy to accept;
But in the gentle art of kindness
    You've been most adept.

DEAR DAD

I seldom take the time to tell you
   All the things I feel.
I want to tell you that my love
   For you is very real.

I'll long appreciate your many
   Kind and thoughtful deeds.
You've always been so sensitive
   Responding to my needs.

I feel that you are special;
   Let me thank you from my heart
For all your treasured wisdom
   And the warmth that you impart.

I always will respect you for
   The ways in which you care.
It's reassuring knowing that
   Your love is always there.

THANK YOU FOR BEING MY PARENT

There is no single way that I could
    Ever rate or rank you,
Except to say that you're the best—
    For having me, I thank you.

Your role as parent merits
    My most special gratitude—
I'll long appreciate your warm
    And loving attitude.

True parenting is more than
    Bringing someone into being
Or giving them a place to stay,
    The basics guaranteeing.

It's setting an example
    That is plain for them to see.
It's knowing when to tell them yes
    Or when to disagree.

It's reaching out to understand
    Their questions and concerns.
It's sensing the security
    For which a child yearns.

It's seeing the commitment
    That good parenting involves.
It's knowing all the problems
    That a loving parent solves.

I'm grateful for the many times
    Your gracious warmth has smiled.
I'll always say with loving thanks—
    I'm glad to be your child.

I'M YOUR PARENT, I'M YOUR FRIEND

In my heart I'm confident
    Two attitudes can blend
So I can always feel that
    I'm your parent, I'm your friend.

I know that our relationship
    Is one we must defend.
Though changes are occurring,
    I'm your parent, I'm your friend.

The differences of generations
    We can both transcend.
Let's always talk together—
    I'm your parent, I'm your friend.

There is a sense of love and warmth
    On which we both depend.
It lets me say with fondness—
    I'm your parent, I'm your friend.

The bond that we have built with time
    Is one that mustn't end.
It must in fact grow stronger—
    I'm your parent, I'm your friend.

YOU'RE MY PARENT, YOU'RE MY FRIEND

You've guided me as parent;
　　On your strength I did depend.
And now as I am growing up,
　　I hope you'll be my friend.

You've helped with many choices;
　　My respect for you endures.
But we must learn to make decisions
　　As our life matures.

Independence is a thing
　　Which everyone must learn.
Through new responsibilities
　　Our freedom we must earn.

Growing up, but not apart,
　　My life with yours can blend.
As I grow older, you can be
　　My parent *and* my friend.

I'll always need a parent
　　On whose shoulder I can rest.
But a parent is a friend
　　Who lets you venture from the nest.

I don't know all the answers,
　　But with your help I can try
To look beyond my treasured home
　　And train my wings to fly.

THANK YOU FOR BELIEVING IN ME

You believed in me when I was searching
    For a true direction.
You sensed when I was full of thought,
    Absorbed with introspection.

You never claimed to know the answers,
    Never posed as right.
You never held that my concerns
    Were ludicrous or trite.

I always knew I sought with you
    The meanings right for me.
The process known as choice
    You always felt was better free.

Your own predispositions
    Weren't at issue, only mine.
My knowledge of myself
    Was most important to define.

While I've pursued the future
    Looking for the proper key,
I've grown in strength and confidence
    Since you've believed in me.

I therefore want to thank you for
    The dreams I now embrace,
For dreams are often delicate
    And easy to erase.

BELIEVE IN YOURSELF

Believe in yourself
    To the depth of your being.
Nourish the talents
    Your spirit is freeing.

Know in your heart
    When the going gets slow
That your faith in yourself
    Will continue to grow.

Don't forfeit ambition
    When others may doubt.
It's your life to live—
    You must live it throughout.

Learn from your errors—
    Don't dwell in the past.
Never withdraw
    From a world that is vast.

Believe in yourself;
    Find the best that is you.
Let your spirit prevail;
    Steer a course that is true.

FOLLOW YOUR HEART

In the depth of your being,
    In a place in the heart,
There are times when your reason
    And feeling must part.

Your logic directs you
    To follow one course,
But your innermost feeling
    Applies a firm force.

When instinct and reason
    Diverge and divide,
You must sometimes respond
    To that feeling inside.

For your heart in the end
    Is a much sterner judge
Of a reason that clings
    To a mind that won't budge.

And since life unfolds
    As the subtlest art,
There are times when you clearly
    Must follow your heart.

YOU'LL FIND THE ANSWER

There's a natural urgent desire
    To find all the answers you can.
The question of where you are going
    You ponder again and again.

Because certain answers elude you
    At various stages you reach,
You often miss one hidden message
    That life may be struggling to teach.

It is that the course of your future
    Resembles a ship in the sea.
The swells of the ocean around you
    May confuse you as you're drifting free.

But if each journey's prior condition
    Is seeing the most distant shore,
Then few journeys would ever be taken—
    Most dreams you would have to ignore.

So remember that distant horizons
    All exceed the fixed range of your sight.
And to make your important discoveries
    You must through life's turbulence fight.

For life is a series of tempests
    Obscuring the vision of some;
But if you can weather them patiently,
    Be assured that the answer will come.

BE DIFFERENT, BUT DON'T BE THE SAME

I sense that you want to be different,
　To follow a path of your own.
In matters of taste and convention
　You want to determine the tone.

There are risks when you try to be different,
　New models that must be embraced.
You end up conforming to standards
　That are drawn from another group's taste.

Though you don't want to bow to convention
　And fill a predictable role,
When you yield to a group and its patterns,
　You're under that one group's control.

So if a distinctive life pattern
　Becomes your legitimate aim,
Be aware that conformity beckons—
　Be different, but don't be the same.

THE ART OF LIVING

Our life is but a canvas—
  We're artists of a kind.
As we apply the brush strokes,
  Life's meaning is defined.

We can play the role of master—
  Fill in details of our own—
Or let the paint flow randomly,
  Let chance decide the tone.

We can choose each color wisely—
  Just as friends are picked with care—
Or let all those around us
  Merely place the colors there.

We can look behind us proudly
  At the stages of our art
Or see a life unfolding
  In which we play little part.

Though our life is but a canvas,
  There is much that we can do
To make it our best work of art—
  And our creation, too.

YOU ARE MY FAMILY

A family is a feeling
That lives within the heart.
Members who belong in spirit
Form its truest part.

There are many different ways
A family unit grows;
Yet there is but a single feeling
That each person knows.

It is the sense of unity,
Of love and common caring.
It is the sense unquestioning
Of nurturing and sharing.

Though life brings many combinations,
One great source of pride
Is that warm togetherness
We treasure deep inside.

WILDFLOWER

Wildflower whispering
    Your message to the air,
Dazzling the emptiness
    With radiance so rare.

Budding youth alone amidst
    The grasses growing tall,
Your beauty, as the flower's,
    Has the power to enthrall.

But though the youth and flower
    May converge in certain ways,
The youth requires company;
    The flower needs no vase.

A wildflower may remain
    Alone and be complete;
But every budding youth would like
    Another youth to meet.

So while the flower can exist
    In nature all alone,
The youth must share its beauty,
    Find another all its own.

OUR LIVES TOUCHED

Love had but a little while,
　　So love made me your friend.
The time thus spared, so briefly shared,
　　Was all love had to lend.

I loved you for that moment
　　When lives did briefly touch.
But in its way love wouldn't say
　　How lasting or how much.

If life gives us another chance,
　　We'll have the time to see
If love will have the patience
　　To favor you and me.

But since we cannot hope to know
　　Just what the future sends,
Let's value what we found together
　　Knowing we were friends.

MY FRIEND, MY LOVER

In inner space our lives embrace;
　　In softness I discover
How you in sheltered moments
　　Have become my friend, my lover.

In secret places love erases
　　The innocence of friends.
In warming ways we touch in praise
　　And closeness never ends.

In vision's eye our looks supply
　　A feast of forms to know.
In sensual disclosure
　　We have nothing left to show.

With intimate intentions,
　　Through mutual desires,
For friendliest of reasons,
　　My heart with yours conspires.

SHARE WITH ME

Share with me your inner world;
   Reveal to me your thinking.
Tell me when your spirits soar,
   Or even when they're sinking.

Share with me your every mood.
   Permit me to explore
Your hopes and aspirations—
   Let me know you to the core.

Share with me your true concerns,
   Perplexities and fears.
Share your strengths and weaknesses...
   And don't conceal your tears.

Share with me your fantasies,
   Your loves and your obsessions.
Let me understand your wants
   And savor your impressions.

Let me know your inner warmth
   And share your inner flame.
Tell me all there is to know,
   And I will do the same.

I ENJOY BEING WITH YOU

I enjoy the time when I'm with you;
    I'm happy when we're talking.
I value all the things we do,
    The quiet moments walking.

So many things are better shared;
    And I'm so glad that we
Find such complete fulfillment in
    Each other's company.

There's more to life when you're around;
    You make me feel alive.
There's nothing I withhold from you;
    With you, my passions thrive.

I'm able to explore my thoughts,
    Relax in freedom found.
The confidence I feel is
    Reassuring and profound.

The moments we're together
    Are such special ones for me,
Because I sense that we exist
    In loving harmony.

IF I SEEM INDEPENDENT

If I seem independent,
    Don't be at all concerned.
I am trying to untangle
    All that I have learned.

I feel somewhat vulnerable,
    A little on my guard.
The end of one relationship
    Can hit you really hard.

It's not that I can't open up
    Or create closer ties;
But there's a portion of myself
    That I must recognize.

As I approach the future,
    I can't disregard the past.
I hope you'll try to understand
    Why I can't move too fast.

I'm wary of dependence;
    I want to stand alone;
I have my own identity;
    I feel that I have grown.

I hope that you'll respect me
    As I struggle hard to be
A person who is sensitive,
    Yet confident and free.

TWO FREE

My independence gives me freedom
   Only to be free;
But freedom tells me there is something
   I alone can't be.

For freedom's very private voice
   Must have a private hearing;
And selfless listening can't be found
   Without two people sharing.

Freedom's body, too, must find
   Through warmth its definition.
Alone its fires turn to cold
   Just wanting recognition.

And freedom's soul must find a match;
   New strength it must inherit.
If freedom grows, it's when it knows
   It's found a kindred spirit.

YOU'RE MORE THAN A FRIEND

I have a special feeling
    That I scarcely comprehend.
In my deepest thoughts I sense
    You're more than just a friend.

I wouldn't want to rush us now
    As friendship we explore;
But there's a growing warmth inside
    That I just can't ignore.

I enjoy our times together—
    We're so comfortable and free.
I think of you when I'm alone—
    I think of you and me.

I feel that we have much to share,
    Warm secrets to uncover.
There is a whole lot more to life
    That we can both discover.

I don't know where we're heading
    Or just where this road will end.
But you're truly someone special
    Who is more than just a friend.

I LOVE YOUR MYSTERY

You're rather unpredictable;
　　You're different, not the same—
A puzzle to decipher,
　　A freest wind to tame.

I never hope to understand
　　Your subtleties and shades.
Each time I chase your meaning,
　　All my comprehension fades.

I never can predict exactly
　　How you're going to act.
The only thing that's constant
　　Is the way that you attract.

I'll never find the answers—
　　All solutions you defy.
But since I love your mystery,
　　It's fun for me to try.

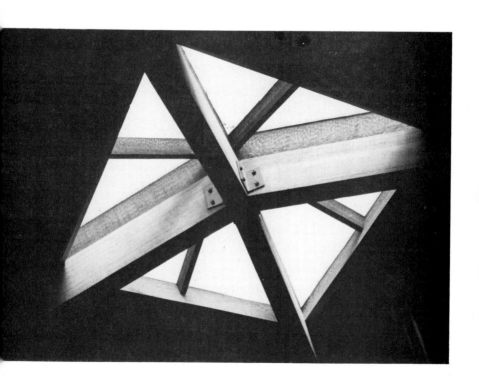

LET'S TAKE OUR TIME

We've got a nice relationship;
    Let's hope that it will last.
But in our haste to know each other
    Let's not go too fast.

An autumn leaf needs time to change
    From green to golden yellow;
A vintage wine needs time to age;
    A love needs time to mellow.

Before we harvest prematurely
    All that love has sown,
Let's find a pace that suits us both
    And wait 'til love has grown.

We both can sense our love's potential
    In the times ahead.
But let's not rush it; let's be patient;
    Let's go slow instead.

I'LL WAIT FOR YOU

I know that you're not ready yet—
    Your love I won't pursue;
But while you're making up your mind,
    My love will wait for you.

A love that's freely chosen
    Is a love that will endure.
A love that is prepared to wait
    Will end up more secure.

My love for you is something
    That I never will outgrow.
I'll wait until you're sure enough
    To answer yes or no.

And if you should decide that love
    Is not for us to share,
I hope that you will tell me so
    And your true thoughts declare.

But if you sense that love describes
    The feeling in your heart,
Then share with me your deepest thoughts
    So we're not long apart.

COME SHARE MY LIFE

I've wandered through the forest
And heard its sounds alone.
I've seen a robin hopping
And paused where moss has grown.

I've thrown a pebble seaward
While walking on the sand.
I've sat and watched the waves break
And gathered shells in hand.

I've seen the autumn colors
And hiked through winter snow.
I've felt the summer rainfall
And watched spring flowers grow.

I've savored life in moments past,
But now I understand—
There's more to life if we can share it
Walking hand in hand.

LEND ME LOVE

Lend me love
  And love me true
And lure me into
  Debt with you.

All the love that
  I can borrow
I'll repay before
  Tomorrow.

To the sum of
  Totals due
I'll add my highest
  Interest, too.

That way my payments
  Will accrue
As functions of
  My love for you.

Each time your heart
  Approves a loan,
I'll reimburse it
  From my own.

TOGETHER

If life is full of challenge
  And gives us outstretched wings,
Let's soar to highest places
  And discover many things...
                              together.

If life reveals its message
  To open eyes and ears,
Let's savor all the beauty
  And conquer any tears...
                              together.

If life is meant for sharing
  And time forever runs,
Let's find our hidden moments
  And chase the setting sun...
                              together.

If life is meant for loving
  And love is meant for two,
Let's never waste a moment
  Nor ever miss a cue...
                              together.

If life is ever lonely
  And two are ever free,
Let us recall the moments
  When life placed you and me...
                              together.

WHEN WE ARE APART

In matters of the heart
    I have a weakness that is clear—
I can't imagine loneliness
    As long as you are near.

But when I can't be with you
    And I'm feeling all alone,
The sense of isolation
    Is the greatest I have known.

While we are close together,
    I am blissfully aware
That I am truly happy
    Merely knowing you are there.

But when we are apart,
    The very opposite is true—
I am totally distracted
    Merely knowing there is you.

I MISS YOU

A little bit of you
　　And a little bit of me
Have switched respective places
　　In a mystifying " we."

When miles come between us
　　And our lives are drawn apart,
Our thoughts remain together
　　Tugging softly at the heart.

This loneliness without you
　　Tells of special moments shared
And says across the miles
　　Just how much we've always cared.

The emptiness that comes
　　With just the memory of your touch
Stirs a feeling from within that says,
　　" I miss you very much."

YOU FILL MY THOUGHTS

In tender ways
    I often find
You fill my thoughts—
    You're on my mind.

In cherished moments
    I can sense
You give my thoughts
    Their eloquence.

In fond reflections
    Through the day
I think of you
    In every way.

In fleeting glimpses
    Of the past
The thoughts of you
    Are those that last.

In times apart
    I've always known
Through thoughts of you
    I'm not alone.

YOU ARE ON MY MIND

Something in my inner space
 Would like to bridge the miles.
Something in the way I miss you
 Seems the worst of trials.

Something in the feelings
 That are kindled in my heart
Stirs the warmth and then the cold
 Of knowing we're apart.

Something in my memory
 That teases me so much
Is trying to recapture
 The true essence of your touch.

Something in the fleeting thoughts
 That merge both joy and pain
Make the passions of the heart
 Much harder to contain.

Something in my quiet moments
 Seems at once so dear
When thoughts of you can crystallize
 Into a joyful tear.

Something in the way the heart
 A ray of warmth can find
Reminds me of just how I feel
 When you are on my mind.

I NEED YOU

It seems you're always in my dreams—
    You fill my waking hours.
Your presence and your promise
    Warm me with their magic powers.

My heart's in disarray—My mind
    Is reeling with distraction.
My body feels for yours
    An irresistible attraction.

Whenever we're apart, that sense
    Of emptiness starts growing.
But when you're close to me
    My world is filled to overflowing.

My thoughts all lead to passion—
    My emotions fully heed you.
Each moment, every bit of me
    Keeps saying that I need you.

YOU'RE MY FANTASY

You are my favored fantasy,
  My island of discovery.
You elevate my spirits—
  You're my reason for recovery.

You stir my fond imaginings,
  Give reverie its fuel.
You brighten every moment—
  You're my ever precious jewel.

You stimulate my senses;
  You're the center of my thinking.
You give me hope and optimism,
  Keep my faith from shrinking.

You tutor me in passion,
  Give substance to my dreams.
You fill up my emotions,
  Let me love you to extremes.

You and I are lovers
  In that land within the heart.
Let's hope it's ours forever;
  Let's hope we'll never part.

LOVE IS A RAINBOW

Love is a rainbow
　Where true colors blend.
You are the treasure
　I find at the end.

Love is our spectrum
　Of thoughts and emotions,
Our feelings of warmth
　And affectionate notions.

Love's our invisible
　Visible force—
Our ultimate, infinite,
　Exquisite source.

Love is our fantasy
　Glimmering bright,
Life's beautiful image
　Reflecting the light.

Love is our dream
　That wants to come true—
I'm glad to be sharing
　This rainbow with you.

WITH YOU, I'M ME

With you I feel that I can be
  Spontaneous and free.
I open up my heart to you
  In simple honesty.

I share with you my inner thoughts,
  Abandon all disguises.
I bare my deepest feelings,
  Shunning pretense or surprises.

I stand before you as I am,
  My strengths and flaws revealed.
No attitudes are hidden;
  No motives are concealed.

With you I'm free to be myself,
  Voice my identity.
I draw from you an inner calm
  That says—with you, I'm me.

WE NEED EACH OTHER

There's a simple mathematics,
So absolute and true,
That says that one and one will always
End up being two.

But there's another set of laws
With love and life its source
That says two lives together
Can unleash a vital force.

I know that we have found this force—
Our spirits truly blend.
We've tapped an inner freedom—
On each other we depend.

We've found that special meaning—
We can cherish every hour.
We've discovered our own formula,
Revealed an inner power—

That chemistry of sharing,
That higher math of hearts
Whose sum of total being
Is much greater than its parts.

SOMETHING HAPPENED IN MY HEART

Something happened in my heart
   A breath or two ago.
Its rhythm skipped and raced a bit
   And caused an inner glow.

I lost a breath as I drew in
   A fleeting thought of you.
I held the thought inside me—
   Then I let it filter through.

The warmth that it awakened,
   The feelings that it stirred
Gently notified me
   Something special had occurred.

For as I drew into my heart
   Your image passing through,
I knew that I had lost a breath
   And skipped a beat for you.

I'M CRAZY OVER YOU

Sometimes I'm crazy, distracted, confounded
    And climbing the walls over you.
No matter the season, the day or the reason,
    These feelings I just can't subdue.

I'm babbling, billowing, bubbling over—
    I'm feeling berserk and unstable.
I can't get a grip on myself or my feelings—
    When I try to calm down, I'm unable.

I'm out of this world with excitement.
    I'm feeling mixed up through and through.
I'm high in the sky and I'm crazy—
    I'm wildly insane about you.

YOU TURN ME ON

I'm a captive,
　　I'm a pawn
To moments when
　　You turn me on.

You stir my senses,
　　Fill my mind,
Unleash my passions,
　　Make me blind.

You're the strongest
　　Of all potions.
You're the key
　　To my emotions.

You will it, want it,
　　Seek it, take it,
Show it, flaunt it,
　　Can't forsake it.

You're an adult;
　　You're a child;
You're the one
　　Who makes me wild!

YOU ARE MY POETRY

An image growing stronger,
    A metaphor increasing,
My source of inspiration,
    You are my love unceasing.

A mood I want to capture,
    A feeling to explore,
A message from inside me,
    A thought I can't ignore.

A need to know you further,
    To let my heart expound,
A hunger to describe the inner
    Beauty I have found.

You are my heart's creation;
    You set my verses free;
You are the words I'm looking for;
    You are my poetry.

HONEYSUCKLE

Honeysuckle satisfaction,
  Honeysuckle savor.
Honeysuckle sense of sweetness,
  Filling me with flavor.

Honeysuckle perfume,
  Unannounced in your seduction,
Floating in so freely,
  Never needing introduction.

Never could I love another
  As I now love you.
No nectar to my lips
  Could match your purity so true.

And once I've sipped your faint aroma
  To intoxication,
No flower less than yours
  Will stir my fond anticipation.

THROUGH OUR EYES

Through my eyes, look into me—
   See things no one has seen.
Gaze a while, see a smile,
   Let nothing come between.
Discover all and then some more;
   Find facets never found.
Let my eyes tell everything
   Without a single sound.

Through your eyes will I perceive
   The infinite in you—
The crystal maze that time surveys
   And life brings into view.
I'll gather in your brightest rays,
   Discover hidden talents;
I'll penetrate the mystery
   Of lives and hearts in balance.

I'll look at you and you at me—
   Our eyes will talk together.
Our meanings will traverse the air
   As softly as a feather.
We'll know the truth that words and deeds
   Don't have the time to tell;
And through our eyes shall I in you
   And you in me e'er dwell.

OUR UNIVERSE

Alone...
>   I looked into the night
>   and felt its cold.

Standing together...
>   We saw the stars
>   and were amazed.

Touching each other...
>   We forgot darkness
>   and discovered our own universe.

Sharing...
>   We explored that universe
>   and found it a warmer, better place.

Loving...
>   We became aware
>   of its infinite depth.

Growing together...
>   We wanted our universe
>   to endure.

Remaining together...
>   We created a beautiful
>   synthesis of our dreams.

YOU ARE MY INSPIRATION

You are my inspiration,
    My source of energy.
You stimulate my senses;
    You set my spirits free.

You liberate my thinking;
    You captivate my heart.
You redefine my vision;
    You magnify my art.

You stir my independence;
    You sentence me for life
To see your sweeter meanings—
    You still the outer strife.

You bring me close to nature;
    You share with me its truth.
You rush me into springtime;
    You exercise my youth.

You make all time seem precious—
    Life's essence you enhance.
You fill my days with wonder
    And exquisite romance.

OUR RELATIONSHIP IS SPECIAL

Our relationship is special;
  Our friendship is the best.
Our love is ever growing;
  Our life's a wondrous quest.

We share all things together;
  We never feel alone.
We look at all we've been through;
  We look at how we've grown.

We grasp the tender moments,
  The times we spend as one.
We savor our accomplishments,
  The projects we've begun.

We think of how much better
  Life flows as you and me.
We can't escape the loving thought
  That we were meant to be.

THE PERFECT TWO

If I define the number *two*,
  There's just one meaning, me and you.
If I explain the pronoun *we*,
  I'm struck with thoughts of you and me.
If I explore the small word *us*,
  I see it lasting ever thus.
If I reflect on life *together*,
  I see no hint of stormy weather.

If there's a chance you share my view
  And see in us the perfect *two*
And feel quite free
  In using *we*
And give a plus
  To dreams of *us*,
Then possibly heart's fragile tether
  Will keep the two of us *together*.

I LOVE YOU

I'm thinking, dreaming,
  Conscious of you,
Feeling, knowing
  That I love you.

I'm sensing, seeing
  How you haunt me,
Wishing, hoping
  That you want me.

I'm noting, minding
  How I heed you,
Contemplating
  That I need you.

I'm witnessing
  Through waves and oceans
How you govern
  My emotions.

No thought I have
  Exists above you.
In my heart I know
  I love you.

YOU AND I

You and I,
    A special phrase,
That warms the night
    And lights the days.

You and I,
    A concept true,
That speaks of love
    And visions new.

You and I,
    A precious time,
A gentle thought,
    A tender rhyme.

You and I,
    Two hearts that care,
Two minds that mesh,
    Two lives that share.

Love and hope
    And sun and sky
Now whisper dreams
    Of you and I.

I'M FEELING CLOSE TO YOU

A message inside me,
  A feeling I know
Is stirring a warm
  And affectionate glow.

I'm feeling so close to you,
  Feeling so near,
That songs from my heart
  Are all that I hear.

Your spirit has drifted
  Right into my dreams.
I'm endlessly seeing
  Your image, it seems.

Our hearts are together;
  Our spirits are free;
We're drifting together
  So effortlessly.

No distance, no freedom
  Can draw us apart.
I'm closer to you where it counts—
  In the heart.

FOR MY LOVE

I searched my world for you...
Uncertain of your existence,
I hoped, but sometimes doubted, that I would find you.
I now feel the pressure lifted.
I look and still see those around me;
But my looking and seeing are an affirmation
Of my discovery of you.
As time passes, the gift of chance that you represent
Becomes even more evident and striking.
The improbability of *us*
As a function of life's chance encounters
Frightens me;
Because if you had not been there when I was,
Or I had not been there when you were,
We wouldn't have found
That miracle of warmth and completeness we now feel.
Were this gift not ours,
Were you not mine,
I would still be searching for you
As a boat in fog seeks its mooring,
As a swimmer his landfall,
As an airborne seed its permanent base of growth.

LOVE IS ALWAYS THERE

The life we lead,
　　The hopes we share
Remind us love
　　Is always there.

When roads we walk
　　Appear uphill,
We demonstrate
　　A patient will.

When life's dilemmas
　　Pass us by,
We celebrate
　　A cloudless sky.

The dullest trip
　　Would always be
On flattest land
　　Or quiet sea.

But how enchanting
　　Is the quest
That sometimes puts us
　　To the test.

And how exciting
　　Is the find
When lives are fondly
　　Intertwined.

I BELIEVE IN US

I believe in thoughts we share,
    In feelings we discuss.
I believe in magic moments—
    I believe in us.

I believe in sunny days,
    The warming touch of rain.
I believe in special times
    That form an endless chain.

I believe in quiet nights,
    In vivid starlit skies.
I believe in tender sights
    That stir romantic eyes.

I believe in positives,
    In truths that form a plus.
I believe in love and sharing—
    I believe in us.

LOVE IS...

Love is finding that with you
    Each simple thing is something new,
Each winter hour is full of spring,
    Each moment is worth cherishing.

It's feeling in your presence free
    And knowing that with you I'm me.
It's finding comfort at your side
    And seeking moments to confide.

It's sensing darkness when you're gone
    Yet knowing night must yield to dawn.
It's feeling snug when we're together
    And finding calm in any weather.

It's feeling youth at every age.
    It's being rich despite your wage.
It's feeling happy, seldom blue;
    But, darling, most of all it's you!

ALL I WANT IS YOU

I'll tell it rather simply;
    I'll say it plain and true—
A single thing is all I want;
    And all I want is you.

There are no other riches,
    No treasures or possessions
That ever could compare with you,
    My fondest of obsessions.

You are the very air I breathe,
    The ration that sustains me.
You're all my thoughts tied up as one,
    The laugh that entertains me.

You're all that life need ever give,
    The maximum that's due.
If I could ask for anything,
    I'd only ask for you.

THE ONE I LOVE

The one I love is all I need
   To set my heart ablaze.
The one I love's the center of
   My life in many ways.

The one I love is part of me,
   Companion to my dreams,
And is the main ingredient
   In all my thoughts, it seems.

The one I love supports me through
   The challenges I face
And knows the healing power
   Of a warm and fond embrace.

The one I love responds to me,
   My spirits can renew.
The one I love is full of passion;
   The one I love is you!

MARRIAGE OF TWO HEARTS

In every heart there is a spark
That wants to be a flame.
In every life there is a part
That only love can tame.

In every day there is a moment
Eager to be shared.
In every mind a tender thought
Just waits to be declared.

In every forest there's a trail
Which two can happier roam.
In every place there is a spot
Which two can call a home.

In every joy a higher gladness
Reigns if there are two.
In every love there is the hope
That dreams will all come true.

In every marriage of two hearts
Two lives exist as one.
In every journey that two share
Life's really just begun.

MY WIFE, MY LOVE

My wife, my love, my dearest friend,
　　You've given me your heart to tend.
I've given you my life to share;
　　My heart is in your tender care.

My wife, my hope, my fondest dream,
　　We form a true devoted team.
In all the moments life may bring,
　　You are my star, my everything.

My wife, my source of lasting truth,
　　You stir in me eternal youth;
You give my heart a sense of pride;
　　You fuel my warmest thoughts inside.

My wife, my daily inspiration,
　　You're the love in my equation.
You're my source of deep affection.
　　You're my compass and direction.

WE HAVE IT ALL

We may at times feel lacking in
    The luxuries of living,
But luxuries cannot compare
    With all that life is giving.

We have our lives together;
    We have our shared affection;
We have the hopes and aspirations
    Of a shared direction.

We have the riches of the heart,
    Of family and friends.
We have respect for one another
    That our loving lends.

We have the comfort of just knowing
    That someone is near.
We have the reassurance
    Of a sympathetic ear.

We have the bounties of each day,
    Events both large and small.
Through all the moments that we share,
    We really have it all.

OUR LOVE

Our love is something we have built
    From passions, hopes and dreams.
It's safe from any passing moods,
    Secure from all extremes.

It's something real and special,
    Something solid, something pure.
It's something we can always count on,
    Ringing sound and sure.

It's something grounded in the heart,
    Emitting confidence.
It lives in our emotions;
    It is something we can sense.

Our love remains a binding force,
    Resistant to all strife.
Amidst the outer pressures,
    It's our anchor throughout life.

I'M SECURE IN YOU

There are things the heart won't question,
　　Sensations so secure,
That they exist in mind and flesh,
　　In primal regions pure.

They have the strength of granite,
　　The softness of a touch,
The full persuasion of a flower,
　　The warmth that means so much.

I cannot take for granted
　　That such treasures are my due.
Instead I'm awed and thankful
　　That I feel secure in you.

Such chemistry does not result
　　From feeble fascination.
It's active; it's dynamic;
　　It needs loving affirmation.

The confidence I feel in you
　　Is my profoundest praise.
My love for you will thrive in me
　　And brighten all my days.

YOU ARE MY STAR

You are my star
    Shining ever so bright.
You walk with the sun;
    You challenge the night.

You guide me through darkness,
    Chase shadows by day.
You force all the problems
    Of living away.

You warm by your presence;
    You lift up my moods.
You raise me in spirit
    To high altitudes.

You light up my thinking;
    You charm every hour.
You summon within me
    A much higher power.

You color my future,
    Cast rainbows afar.
You're my stellar body—
    Yes, you are my star.

YOU'RE PERFECT IN MY EYES

Like clouds across the sunset,
    A moon in starry skies,
A rainfall in the springtime—
    You're perfect in my eyes.

All beauty has its shades and tones,
    Each gem a form that's raw.
Each diamond has a subtle way
    Of mirroring its flaw.

I see you as the misty mask
    Enshrouding early day.
I see you as the wildflower
    Nuzzling grass away.

I see you as a naked form
    With memory's lonely scars.
I see you as a feeling
    That no inner knowledge mars.

I see you as temptation
    Casting off your scant disguise.
I see you as a natural—
    You're perfect in my eyes.

A TIME FOR US

In a little space amidst the hurry
   Where the world is free of fuss,
Let's share a moment all our own—
   A special time for us.

Let's shape a quiet interlude,
   Explore our inner being.
Let's see ourselves as only we
   Are capable of seeing.

Let's rediscover hidden moments,
   Times of you and me.
Let's recreate the moods we've known,
   So sensuous and free.

Let's bring our lives together,
   Find the warmth that means so much.
Let's draw our beating hearts so close
   That they can almost touch.

And after hearts have spoken
   And this special time has fled,
A silent closeness, calm and sure,
   Will fill our hearts instead.

I WANT YOU

In a peaceful, perfect moment,
In a mood of gentle giving,
Let's flow into each other,
Turn each other on to living.

In a free and open manner,
In a ritual of senses,
Let's cast off inhibition
And abandon our defenses.

In a scene of sensuality,
In the confidence of sharing,
Let's tease and touch and tantalize
And be a little daring.

In the fullest self-expression,
In the peace of perfect pleasure,
Let's fuse our hearts together
And explore love's tender treasure.

HAPPY BIRTHDAY, SWEETHEART

This day was meant for you, my love—
    You're all that I am thinking of.
There's nothing I would rather do
    Than spend this special time with you.

Your birthday will fond memories fill;
    But in our feelings time stands still.
Our life together turns a page;
    But in our hearts love has no age.

Togetherness is our true vow—
    We're living in a sacred now.
We value all the things we share—
    Our perfect space is everywhere.

This birthday wish tells how I feel—
    My love for you is very real.
It seems the proper time to say—
    I love you, dear, in every way.

THAT ENERGY CALLED LOVE

That physical focus,
  That river of heart,
That moment of mutual
  Magical art.

The tactile encounter,
  The total surrender,
The feeling of fusion,
  The sipping of splendor.

The tasting and testing,
  The trying and trading,
The helping, assisting,
  Exploring and aiding.

The limitless loving,
  The endless profusion,
The sensuous searching,
  Defying conclusion.

The energy flooding,
  The warmth overflowing,
The passion expanding,
  The dialog growing.

That moment, that minute—
  Obsessive, unending—
When the energy found in two lovers
  Is blending.

STAY CLOSE TO ME

When morning sun is beaming
   On our silhouetted love
And as I stir I know that
    You are all I'm thinking of,
                Stay close to me.

When birds commence their songs of love
   And sound their soft alarm
And, lacking inhibition,
    We are tangled arm in arm,
                Stay close to me.

When comfort streams between two bodies
    Welded side to side
And when there are no secrets
    For familiar forms to hide,
                Stay close to me.

When touching is a tactile treasure
    We can both explore
And we can sense each other's
    Inner appetite for more,
                Stay close to me.

When love's a true collaboration,
    Perfect with its flaws,
A joy that needs elaboration,
    Thriving "just because,"
                Stay close to me.

When every mood we share
    Is but an exercise in love
And two unique identities
    Can fit just like a glove,
                Stay close to me.

When we can still experiment,
    Discover something new,
And all the mystery of love
    Is there when I'm with you,
                Stay close to me.

When we can watch the setting sun
    With optimistic eyes
And learn to love the night
    Before the sun begins to rise,
                Stay close to me.

I LOVE YOU MORE EACH DAY

I saw you again today
   For the first time.
Love, you see, has a way of letting us
   Rediscover yesterday's surprises.

Tomorrow, I'll again be alert to you—
   Your words, your appearance,
   Your movement, your touch—
For I'm certain there's something
   I missed today.

Each day I want to discover
   All there is to discover;
But each succeeding day
   My discovery begins anew.

PLEASE SAVE SOME TIME FOR ME

The time we share has grown too scarce;
Our special moments flee.
Though life has its required tasks,
Please save some time for me.

There are so many routine things
To occupy our days
It's often hard to meet within
The center of our maze.

We give a lot of extra effort
To the things we do
And often spend our energies
Alone and not as two.

And when our first free moment
Then becomes a date to keep,
Our need to share competes with our
More basic need for sleep.

My batteries need charging;
I'm short of energy.
I want to share my life with you—
Please save some time for me.

I NEED A HUG

At the end of a lengthy
  And tiring day
When I've faced the world
  In my private way,
                    I need a hug!

When I'm hungry and cranky
  And feeling up tight
And a day has just passed
  When too little went right,
                    I need a hug!

When my body is craving
  The warmth of another
And my poor aching muscles
  Compete with each other,
                    I need a hug!

When I'm insecure
  And a little bit nutty
And my mind is exhausted,
  My body like putty,
                    I need a hug!

When I am affectionate,
  Loving and caring
And want to enjoy
  A real moment of sharing,
                    I need a hug!

I'M SENSITIVE TO YOU

I'm influenced in many ways
    By things you say and do.
I guess, to put it simply,
    I am sensitive to you.

This means that deep inside my heart
    I've made a conscious choice
To weigh your words with care
    And know each nuance of your voice.

This is the highest compliment,
    The truest sign of love.
It shows that as I live my life
    You're what I'm thinking of.

In giving you complete and total
    Access to my heart,
I focus in on certain feelings
    You alone impart.

This means your words will always have
    A powerful effect.
I may react to things you say
    In ways you don't expect.

I hope that you will understand
    We have so much to share.
If ever I react to you,
    It's just because I care.

LOVE MAKES IT WORK

We needn't pretend that it's perfect,
   Nor dwell on the fact that it's not.
We needn't expect a relationship
   Devoid of all blemish or spot.

It's normal to be a bit human:
   Some problems are part of the game.
Things would be hopelessly boring
   If, flawlessly, we were the same.

But still it's important to notice,
   No matter how human we are,
That love is the measure of progress:
   It leads us and guides us afar.

We don't have to worship perfection,
   Nor give up all struggle for change;
But love can be perfect when we're not—
   It's a gift we can proudly exchange.

WE'RE A COUPLE OF NUTS

Some love is pure and simple,
　　Rather free of stress and strain.
Other loves are rarely quiet,
　　Borderline insane.

Instead of a relationship
　　That's dull and ordinary,
Ours is highly volatile
　　And often adversary.

Our love requires conflict
　　To perform its very best.
Our love is one that thrives upon
　　The highest form of test.

Though another couple
　　Might find normal stress combatible,
We are never satisfied
　　Unless we're incompatible.

While others use endearments
　　To uplift them from a rut,
We unleash terse phrases such as
　　"Pain in the old butt."

The strange admission we must make
　　Is that it all seems right.
If we didn't have each other,
　　Whom would we then fight?

For B. and L.

LET'S RELAX

Let's make a pact and take a vow
  That goes into effect right now
That when our aggravation peaks
  Because of certain hectic weeks,
                    We'll just relax.

When we try hard to understand
  What others want and some demand
And, striving to impress another,
  We fail to understand each other,
                    Let's just relax.

When certain rather touchy dealings
  Force us to suppress our feelings
And as we try to do things right
  We end up feeling more up tight,
                    Let's just relax.

When we all try to do too much
  And life seems tender to the touch
And being perfect is our goal
  And little feeds our heart and soul,
                    Let's just relax.

When schedules are always full
  And there's just time for push and pull
And warmth and closeness seem to be
  A scarce but all important key,
                    Let's just relax.

WE'RE UNDER A LOT OF STRESS

We're strong and we're close
    And we're loving and caring—
Our relationship's solid,
    Our lives meant for sharing.

But sometimes the pressures of life
    Appear greater.
We want them to vanish
    Right now and not later.

When things grow too tense
    And we're short with each other,
We sometimes forget
    How we love one another.

Whenever this happens,
    We both must confess
Our love's not in danger;
    We're just under stress.

The things that we say
    And the things that we feel
Are spurred on by pressure
    And not always real.

Whenever such tensions
    Put us to the test,
We can't help but realize—
    Our love is the best.

I'M FEELING A LITTLE LONELY

I sometimes want to hear
    The warm expressions of your heart;
But if you wait for me to speak,
    We may not always start.

I sometimes want to feel your touch
    And sense your passion growing;
But if your touch depends on mine,
    Such moments we're forgoing.

I sometimes hope you'll sense my needs
    And let my needs compel you;
But when you don't respond to me,
    I'm lonely and can't tell you.

I sometimes hope you'll understand
    How oft my spirit yearns
To know that in another heart
    An equal fire burns.

I sometimes hope you'll let my heart
    Bring all its warmth to living;
But every heart must sometimes take
    Before it turns to giving.

LOVE IS A WORD

Love is a word
　With a sensible sound,
Yet its use makes a sensible
　Head go around.

For it seems that this word
　Can have multiple uses
Which sometimes can lead
　To more subtle abuses.

This says to a sensitive,
　Critical heart
That the language of love
　Is a language apart.

The use of the word
　Affords no real assurance
That the feeling behind it
　Has chance of endurance.

So love can't depend
　On an audible sound,
For the silence of love
　Is a silence profound;

And the actions that help
　In defining this word
Go beyond any message
　So easily heard.

LET'S MAKE IT WORK

Our relationship is strong enough
    To weather any test.
With conscious effort we can strive
    To make our love the best.

If we can only empathize
    With one another's feelings
And learn to talk out differences
    Without our thoughts concealing,

We'll prove that in those periods
    Of tensions overflowing
Our hearts are patient through it all—
    Our love is ever growing.

If we can stress the positive,
    Not magnify the worst,
We'll focus on each other's strengths
    And see the good things first.

If we can see the brighter side
    Through every shade of weather,
We'll have the confidence to say:
    Let's make it work together.

I NEED TIME TO THINK

In this moment of uncertainty
   When my thoughts are filled with doubt,
I need to spend some time alone—
   I need to think it out.

I need to re-examine
   Every feeling I can find.
I need to grasp and then untangle
   All that's on my mind.

I need to look into my heart
   And see just where I stand.
I need to find the meaning of
   The things we've shared and planned.

I'll search for what's important;
   Past and present I will link.
I'll try to understand us more—
   I just need time to think.

WE NEED TO TALK

I've done a lot of thinking
    And would welcome your suggestions
As to how we can approach
    Some rather disconcerting questions.

Can we still be sure
    That our relationship is growing?
Is it real or just a habit;
    Where's our love now going?

Should we strive to give it life,
    Pay more attention to it?
How much longer can we need to talk
    And still not do it?

I think it's time that we discuss
    Just where our love is heading.
Sincerity and candor
    Will be healthy, not upsetting.

If our love is worth preserving,
    Surely we will know.
If love is what we're still deserving,
    Clearly it will show.

I NEED TO TALK IT OUT

Sometimes I react to things
    Internally and strongly,
Especially when someone very close
    Has acted wrongly.

To keep emotions pent up
    When another acts unkind
Gnaws at my emotions
    And disturbs my peace of mind.

There is a mental tyranny
    Some wield at closest range
That makes the heart rebellious
    And desirous of change.

There's but a single answer
    When you're hurting to the core;
You must release the deep emotions
    That you tend to store.

Therefore, I must talk it out
    And let my feelings flow.
It's not healthy to repress them—
    Someone has to know.

I can't always be so tactful,
    Subtle or discreet.
I have feelings I must share
    For me to be complete.

IT'S TIME TO OPEN UP

You never have to tell me
    Just what is on your mind.
Your feelings can go undiscussed,
    Your problems undefined.

You never have to open up
    And tell me your concerns.
I can't compel you to discuss
    Why your behavior turns.

Your private thoughts
    Are your domain;
You may reserve
    Your joys and pain.

But if you feel
    You really care,
There are some meanings
    You must share.

And if our friendship
    Is to grow,
Your subtleties
    I'd like to know.

You must reveal
    What's in your heart
To let our deeper
    Feelings start.

For us to drink
    From friendship's cup,
It's time for us
    To open up.

LET ME UNDERSTAND YOU

Let me understand you;
  Let me step inside your mind.
Let me try to comprehend
  The puzzles that I find.

Let me be compassionate
  And sensitive and caring
And always show a deep concern
  For how your life is faring.

And as I struggle at the task
  Of understanding you,
I hope that you will not forget
  That I am human, too.

For it's quite easy to become
  Obsessed with one's own plight
And miss the point that others also
  Wage a lonely fight.

So as you strive to understand
  What life is all about,
You'll benefit if you can sense
  The need for reaching out.

For as your focus broadens,
  It will mean that you have grown;
You'll better understand yourself
  And seldom be alone.

I TRUSTED YOU

Often we must act on faith
  And trust another's word.
We must make a judgment
  On the truth of what we've heard.

This decision may be based
  On insufficient facts.
We may never know just how
  Another person acts.

Still we have a sense of hope
  That decency will rule.
We are optimistic
  That we won't be made a fool.

Promises, however,
  May be made with little thought;
And in the web of careless comments
  Innocence is caught.

Though we may believe
  A person's character is strong,
There are certain moments
  When we know that we were wrong.

YOU LET YOUR REAL SELF SHOW

There's a facet of your being
   That I never got to know
Until that recent moment
   When you let your real self show.

I knew there was a part of you
   I didn't understand,
A thing that made it hard
   For our relations to expand.

I knew it was essential
   That I understand you more
And see your image clearer
   Than I ever had before.

Until that candid moment
   When you voiced your truest feeling,
I only had the slightest hint
   Of what you'd been concealing.

But as you let your feelings out
   And I observed the flow,
I knew I'd seen another you—
   You let your real self show.

NOBODY IS PERFECT

Perfection is a trait
    With all the power to entice;
And those attracted to it
    Have to struggle to be nice.

They place unreal demands upon
    Themselves and others near.
They act as though they listen
    But they seldom ever hear.

They focus on each shortfall,
    And they seldom see the good.
They find no cause for satisfaction
    Even though they should.

They hide their own frustration,
    Often lashing out in haste.
Their highest expectations
    Lead to comments in poor taste.

A person of this disposition
    Always should think twice
And, casting out the negatives,
    Should exercise the nice.

For in the search for perfect features
    No one has begun
Until they recognize
    That human tolerance is one.

PLEASE BE PATIENT WITH ME

I'm going through a period
Of difficult transition.
Life has placed me in a rather
Difficult position.

My mind and mood are going through
A period of stress.
My present and my future
I am trying to assess.

Life is not as smooth and even
As it's been before.
I've got to find direction,
Life's alternatives explore.

I've got to straighten out my life
And struggle to adjust.
I've got to realign my purpose,
Redefine my thrust.

I can't be captive to the past
Or slave to moments lost.
I can't mourn the lessons learned
Or fret about their cost.

As I approach the future,
There is much I can't foresee.
I hope you'll try to understand—
I hope you'll bear with me.

I ACTED WITHOUT THINKING

I acted without thinking
  And behaved a bit unwise.
In looking back I feel that I should
  Now apologize.

I yielded to the moment,
  Rushing to the wrong conclusion.
The words and deeds resulting
  Caused unhappiness, confusion.

Sometimes we move in haste
  Without examining the facts
And launch ourselves into
  The most unfortunate of acts.

I feel that I reacted
  In a manner I regret.
This clearly was a moment
  I'd be happy to forget.

But since I can't go back in time
  And past mistakes ignore,
I'd like to say I'm sorry
  And apologize once more.

I'M SORRY

For things I might have said to you
   In anger or frustration,
For times when words of mine have been
   A source of provocation,
         ...I'm sorry.

For unkind actions, thoughtless deeds
   Or inconsideration,
For jumping to conclusions,
   For rejecting moderation,
         ...I'm sorry.

For timely things I haven't done,
   Forgetting or omitting,
For knowing sometimes I was wrong
   Without, in fact, admitting,
         ...I'm sorry.

For conversations we have had
   When temper stole affection,
For looking in a negative,
   Not positive, direction,
         ...I'm sorry.

For being too insensitive
   And just a bit unwise,
For failing to perceive the need
   For loving compromise,
         ...I'm sorry.

DON'T PLACE ME ON A PEDESTAL

I shouldn't be put on a pedestal—
　　Don't place me where I don't belong.
Don't label me perfect, infallible—
　　Such labels will always prove wrong.

By placing me higher than normal,
　　By making me taller than tall,
You create a strong possibility
　　That I will eventually fall.

I'll never fulfill your high standards
　　Though my private goals I pursue.
Remember I'm trying my hardest;
　　Remember that I'm human, too.

I may not meet your expectations—
　　I'm struggling hard to meet mine.
My life can't be lived by another—
　　My life is for me to define.

For warmth and compassion I'm grateful;
　　Your loving concern is the best.
But if I am placed on a pedestal,
　　I may not arise to the test.

LET'S COMMUNICATE

Let's never underestimate
   Our power to communicate.
If pressures lead to words unfair,
   Let's talk it over, clear the air.
If dialogue can save the day,
   Let's seek the words and find a way.
If inner thoughts are stirring doubt,
   Let's care enough to talk it out.
So silence cannot barriers build,
   Let's keep our lives discussion-filled.
So we don't burst with things unsaid,
   Let's practice speaking out instead.
So we can both feel good inside,
   Let's know we always can confide.
So tender thoughts don't slip the mind,
   Let's always share a word that's kind.
So love is nourished day by day,
   Let's speak our hearts in every way.

A TIME FOR UNDERSTANDING

There are times when each of us
    Runs short of understanding
And we succumb to pressures
    Caused by routines so demanding.

It may be something minor
    With solution just in reach
Or something with a history
    That brings about the breach.

But in the trying situations
    Life holds out for us
We sometimes reach the end of
    What we calmly can discuss.

If we could just reverse the clock,
    The past we could undo;
And in a less upsetting manner
    We could start anew.

But since the past must stay with us,
    Let's redirect our minds
And, valuing the future,
    Look ahead and not behind.

Let's keep all disagreement
    From so needlessly expanding.
Let's focus all our energies
    On better understanding.

LET'S FORGIVE AND FORGET

Let's leave the past
    And live for now.
Our old disputes
    Let's disavow.

Let's make an effort
    To forgive.
Let's look ahead
    And start to live.

Let's never dredge up
    Days completed
And hear the old
    Complaints repeated.

The past is gone—
    The future's here.
Our sores and wounds
    Will disappear.

There's much to gain
    If we forget it.
Life turns a corner
    If we let it.

LET'S PUT IT BEHIND US

Clearly there is something
That is getting in the way.
We are less spontaneous,
Not sure of what to say.

Sometimes there is little
That will satisfy the mind.
Though we search, there are no proper
Comments we can find.

It serves no purpose to probe deeper,
Strive to understand.
Finding fault will not
A firm relationship expand.

Sometimes little things
Can overtake and even blind us.
Sometimes certain things
We'd better take and put behind us.

CAN'T WE JUST BE FRIENDS

You're clearly a person I value—
 I want you to know that I care.
But some things are not meant to happen;
 Some moments aren't meant to be there.

It's not that we can't talk together,
 Exchanging our hopes and our feelings.
But not every innocent contact
 Must lead to more intimate dealings.

There's room in this world to be friendly—
 You're certainly one I respect.
But I have the right to determine
 How closely our lives intersect.

Relationships tend to develop
 As two hearts draw near and unite.
But there is a firm precondition—
 We both have to feel that it's right.

LET'S STILL BE FRIENDS

For a time we were together,
  Sharing life with one another.
We formed a close relationship,
  Then drifted from each other.

We tried our best to make it work—
  We hoped our love would grow;
But the differences between us
  Helped erase love's early glow.

Without the sense of deep commitment
  On which love depends,
We have the choice of closing doors
  Or simply being friends.

Let's hope that breaking up is not
  A time for last goodbyes
And we can find the basis for
  Sincere and friendly ties.

For when you've shared as much as we have,
  Something in you sends
A message to a saddened heart
  And says, "Let's still be friends."

LET'S BE GRACIOUS IN PARTING

Though life together seemed to us
    A journey well worth starting,
We're learning more about each other
    Now that we are parting.

While building a relationship
    Is difficult at best,
The way in which we separate
    Gives decency its test.

It's possible to disagree
    On matters fundamental
Yet still break ties between us
    In a manner that is gentle.

The hurt is going to be with us
    As we adjust to change,
But let's not make it any worse
    As lives we rearrange.

We may or may not need each other
    In the paths we're charting;
But let's be noble, let's be gracious
    In this time of parting.

LOVE WAS UNKIND TO YOU

Though love seemed the answer
    As your lives combined,
I'm sorry you now feel
    That love wasn't kind.

Two hearts draw together
    Fulfilling a need
And every relationship
    Wants to succeed.

But mere optimism
    And vigorous hope
Do not always mean
    That two people can cope.

There's an unspoken wisdom
    That lives in the heart
That says that some people
    Together must part.

Love is a feeling
    That must involve two.
When one heart is closed,
    That is clearly too few.

When two hearts confess
    To a lingering doubt,
One way or another
    They must work it out.

But when it appears
    There's no answer to find,
There's just one conclusion...
    That love's been unkind.

OUR FAMILY HAS CHANGED

Life brings many changes
  To the family as we know it.
Through each ordeal, though love is real,
  It's often hard to show it.

As family members who are asked
  To share in this transition,
We occupy a sensitive
  And difficult position.

The present situation
  Calls for love and understanding.
It isn't easy to adapt
  To changes so demanding.

We must preserve old meanings
  Yet accept and grasp the new.
The love we've known must always be,
  And grow still stronger, too.

And just remember there's one thing
  As constant as the seasons—
That you can count on me
  At any time for any reasons.

I WANT YOU BACK

Something in me can't ignore
How much I really miss you.
Something in me can't forget
How once it felt to kiss you.

Something in the way we talked,
The hopes and times we shared,
Reminds me that in our own way
We loved and, yes, we cared.

Something keeps repeating
There are good times still ahead.
Something in my heart feels
There are fond words to be said.

Something in me senses
We've passed through the darkest weather.
Something keeps on saying
Why can't we get back together.

I CARE FOR YOU

The moods of my mind
   Softly whisper and weave,
And the message I'm hearing
   Refuses to leave...
             I care for you.

In a world that is changing,
   As old patterns shift,
There's a recurrent meaning,
   A general drift...
             I care for you.

No incidents past
   Or memories now
Can silence the feelings
   That my thoughts allow...
             I care for you.

Relationships change
   And people do, too;
But a constant emotion
   Keeps filtering through...
             I care for you.

LET'S BLAME IT ON THE PAST

Let's count the reasons why we are
   The way we are today.
Let's wallow in excuses,
   Find the cause for our dismay.

Let's justify our failings,
   Find the reasons for our faults.
Let's focus on the many ways
   The outer world assaults.

Let's find the explanations,
   Know the source of all our woes,
Explain away bad habits
   And of all our guilt dispose.

We're clearly not responsible;
   No blame can come our way.
The past provides the answers—
   It gets longer every day!

I AM MAD AT NOTHING

I am mad at nothing,
  And nothing's mad at me.
I am simply furious
  At how life seems to be.

I have no cause nor reason,
  No lasting rationale.
But if I need to speculate
  To find a gripe, I shall.

Others seem to share my feelings—
  No one disagrees.
In the midst of tranquil thoughts,
  My peaceful nature flees.

Life creates adversity
  With motives pure and strong.
Life is full of problems
  Even when there's nothing wrong.

I'M ONLY HUMAN

When everybody wants their special
   Problems solved at once
And I must play the genius
   To avoid the role of dunce,
              ...I'm only human!

When twenty projects must be done
   And I've got time for two
And with distractions only one
   Is all that I can do,
              ...I'm only human!

When tasks require concentration
   And complete perfection
And I am being pulled
   In every possible direction,
              ...I'm only human!

When schedules are meant
   For super heroes and magicians
And miracles are needed
   Under optimal conditions,
              ...I'm only human!

When in those moments hectic
   Some are sounding the alarm
And I'm expected to preserve
   My humor and my charm,
              ...I'm only human!

I NEED SOME TIME FOR MYSELF

I need to find some time for me
And gently place upon the shelf
The cares that so absorb the rest—
I need a moment for myself.

I need a brief exemption
From the many tasks of life.
I need an able substitute
To stand and face the strife.

I need an understudy
As chief officer and slave,
A person who by gracious deeds
My sanity can save.

I need the perfect person
Who can occupy my shoes
And do my routines flawlessly
And no good humor lose.

I need a conscientious soul,
Part saint and partly fool;
But how could I enlist such help?
I'd never be so cruel.

THINGS WILL GET BETTER

When things aren't going well for you
    And times aren't what they should be,
Just focus on the positive
    And think about what could be.

Acknowledge what has happened—
    Don't lose sight of lessons past—
But don't allow the negative
    Distracting thoughts to last.

Take what you've learned and start from there;
    Draw strength from your frustration;
And let this added sense of purpose
    Be your new foundation.

It's hard to follow any plan
    Precisely to the letter.
Though life right now is difficult,
    Things will in time get better.

THAT STRENGTH FROM WITHIN

When problems beset us
    Or trials begin,
Let's summon that power,
    That strength from within.

It's there when we need it;
    It flows from the heart.
It's the noblest energy
    Life can impart.

It says: Never weaken—
    Don't ever give in.
With invincible spirit
    Keep striving to win.

Though the odds may seem heavy
    And the effort seem great,
The courage we muster
    Will govern our fate.

So, acknowledge the challenge—
    Then give it your best.
Let that strength from within
    Help you meet every test.

LIFE ISN'T ALWAYS EASY

Life has its trials and obstacles,
  Its measure of setbacks and spills.
Life has its true disappointments,
  Its mountains that start out as hills.

Sometimes we can't find the answers.
  Often we end up depressed.
Frequently we have the feeling
  That life is a terrible test.

Simple solutions elude us.
  Difficult questions remain.
Thought is a lingering burden,
  A well of emotional pain.

Nevertheless there's a dignity
  That we eventually find,
Born of a growing awareness
  Of victories won in the mind.

No battles can ever be greater
  Than those that may never be won.
The fact that you've gallantly struggled
  Is one fact that can't be undone.

The past is a bundle of memories
  Infusing the present with tears.
But you are that person courageous
  Who valiantly still perseveres.

IT'S HOW YOU COPE

Life has its measure of setbacks—
Some are small, some are larger in size.
There are portions of every existence
Which clearly we'd like to revise.

But stresses and problems are normal—
Disappointments are part of the game.
If we let these moments control us,
We must assume part of the blame.

It's how we react that's important;
We mustn't distort what we feel.
Let's work with what life has to offer
And never begrudge a bad deal.

Depression can never assist us
In weathering woes on this earth.
We shouldn't let each disappointment
Give rise to more grief than it's worth.

Instead we should try to discover,
As life in intensity mounts,
A way to place things in proportion.
You see, how we cope is what counts.

IF YOU HAVE A PROBLEM

If you have a problem
    That bothers you inside
And time does little to assure you
    That it will subside,

Then draw upon your inner strength
    And formulate a plan;
And every time you think you can't,
    Remember that you can.

Listen to your deepest voice
    Where reason still remains,
And take control of your own life
    To minimize the strains.

Strip away the fantasies,
    The negatives, the doubts,
The anger, the hostility,
    And guilt's recurrent bouts.

Try to shift into a course
    That's positive in tone.
Communicate your feelings
    So that you are not alone.

A pattern of improvement
    Is the change that you'll be winning
If you'll just let a single step
    Become a new beginning.

LET'S MAKE THE MOST OF LIFE

Let's learn enough about ourselves
 To make a wise concession
And give up habits of the mind
 That lead us to depression.

Life's positives and negatives
 Are shaped by our perception.
To focus on the worst is nothing
 More than self-deception.

How much we make of life
 Is largely based on attitude:
Each moment lets us celebrate
 Or gives us cause to brood.

It's just as easy to perceive
 The world with all its light
As dwell upon the shadows
 And the ebb and flow of night.

The setting sun inspires awe
 Or leads us to despair:
If we but search for beauty,
 Life's full colors will be there.

I BELIEVE IN YOU

The challenges you now confront
    In all you're going through
Help me see the many ways
    That I believe in you.

It's hard for me to realize
    The things that you must face;
And though I try I can't completely
    Step into your place.

But something in my knowledge
    Of the depth and soul of you
Gives to every real concern
    An optimistic hue.

For when you must respond to life
    With pure determination,
Your answer to the challenge
    Is a source of inspiration.

And though each day's uncertainty
    The future oft obscures,
My hope for you is strong
    And my belief in you endures.

YOU CAN MAKE A DIFFERENCE

You can make a difference
In your corner of the earth.
You can reach for higher goals,
Encourage human worth.

You can help the others
To accomplish all they should.
You can find a way
To reinforce the cause of good.

You can try to understand
The problems of the few.
You can be a voice of kindness
Gently passing through.

You can search for purpose
In the many tasks of man.
If you choose to make a difference,
You're the one who can.

FOLLOW YOUR DREAMS

If while pursuing distant dreams
    Your bright hopes turn to gray,
Don't wait for reassuring words
    Or hands to lead the way.

For seldom will you find a soul
    With dreams the same as yours.
Not often will another help you
    Pass through untried doors.

If inner forces urge you
    To take a course unknown,
Be ready to go all the way,
    Yes, all the way alone.

That's not to say you shouldn't
    Draw lessons from the best;
Just don't depend on lauding words
    To spur you on your quest.

Find confidence within your heart
    And let it be your guide.
Strive ever harder toward your dreams
    And they won't be denied.

IF YOU NEVER TRY

If you never try,
   You'll never have to face defeat.
If you never run a race,
   You'll never lose a heat.

If you never stretch your talents,
   You won't risk a tear.
If you never take a chance,
   The odds you'll never fear.

But if you have a lifelong wish
   And you don't venture out,
You will never overcome
   Uncertainty and doubt.

And if you have a goal to reach
   And time is passing by,
You will never know fulfillment
   If you never try.

TAKE CHARGE OF YOUR LIFE

If you feel that life is getting
    Out of your control
And you are just existing
    With no trace of plan or goal,

Don't feel that you're alone
    In your uncertainty and strife;
Work hard to find a better course—
    Take charge of your own life.

Don't wallow in the currents
    Of a life without direction.
Don't tolerate a mental state
    Of crippling introspection.

Don't be a helpless passenger
    Of random circumstance.
Become the driver in your life,
    The governor of chance.

Don't ever act abruptly
    Or proceed without a plan;
If you but have a goal to reach,
    There is a chance you can.

The range of future choices
    Always will appear quite large;
But you will have a greater say
    If you will just take charge.

THE GOAL

The goal is there for all to see—
    The measure of the game.
We're on the field somewhere between
    The failure and the fame.

We try our best to move the ball
    Through patterns, plays and passes.
The goal seems near or far away
    Through our subjective glasses.

The game may be an endless quest,
More losses than advances.
The goal may always loom right there
Eluding all our chances.

We may not ever cross the line;
We may not win the praise;
We may not see our struggles end,
Nor see triumphant days.

But better to have sought the challenge,
Better to have tried,
Better to have found the courage
Dwelling deep inside.

The people from the sidelines
May judge harshly each mistake;
But should you snare the victory
They'll share the winner's cake.

So better risk a contest lost
Than brood of skills forsaken.
The victories will only come
When challenges are taken.

The energy it takes to quell
Ambitions from within
Is often more than it would take
To grab the ball and win.

So if we summon from our hearts
Those strengths we seldom use,
We'll be a victor in the toughest
Contest, win or lose!

I'M PROUD OF YOU

In many ways I'm proud of you—
    You've come a long, long way.
The growth in your abilities
    Has struck me day by day.

Each person has a goal to reach,
    A place they'd like to be,
A standard they aspire for,
    Results they'd like to see.

Some contests are for glory,
    Putting trophies on the shelf.
Others are the ones we wage
    For bettering the self.

It's not the stakes that count, but rather
    How we sense our movement;
And you are on a steady course
    Of rapid self-improvement.

The progress you are showing
    Makes me want to say aloud:
I'm happy where you're going,
    And you make me very proud.

THE GIFT NOT TAKEN

That vapor known as talent
    May induce a certain lift
In one who chooses to acknowledge
    His or her own gift.

But any talent growing
    May be rudely intercepted
If the fact of its existence
    Is too readily accepted.

It's clear and unmistakable
    How total and how swift
Is the loss of any talent
    That too soon is called a gift.

For a talent is a license
    To continue working harder.
By taking it as gift,
    Its precious substance you will barter.

By seeing it as something
    That will never be forsaken,
A gift that is received too soon
    May be a gift not taken.

WHAT IS SUCCESS?

Success is measured day by day—
   It's life that's lived, not squandered.
It's problems solved, meanings found,
   And not just futures pondered.

It's sorting out our hopes and dreams
   From visions all too fleeting.
It's choosing goals within our means,
   Not projects self-defeating.

It's loving self and others, too;
   It's finding peace in duty.
It's sensing harmony in life
   And seeing nature's beauty.

It's living life for all it's worth,
   Not fearful of tomorrow.
It's accepting all that's gone before,
   Not dwelling in past sorrow.

Success is measured not by wealth;
   It's there for rich or poor.
For all who give each day their best
   It leaves an open door.

HAPPINESS

When happiness comes
It comes in a song
With lyrics quite simple
And not very long.

If the tune seems elusive
Don't force it to flow;
When happiness comes
Your heart will know.

The melody's simple;
The words form with ease—
Life's magical moments
Provide all the keys.

Just cherish the beauty
Each moment is bringing—
You'll find that you're suddenly
Happily singing.

FISHERMAN'S LAW

Life is like the sport of fishing—
    A bit of waiting, a bit of wishing,
A constant striving for the prize
    While catching fish of lesser size.

Fishing's like the game of living,
    Sometimes taking, sometimes giving;
Stirring hope while teaching patience;
    Handing out its varied rations.

Though life and fishing have their shoals,
    They lure us with their higher goals.
In life or sport it always seems
    We're happiest among our dreams.

SUCCESS

You can measure success in terms of the past,
  Noting chances you've seized or have wasted.
By just looking back, you can linger in memories
  Of fortunes you've missed or have tasted.

You can measure success in terms of the future—
  Elusive, forever tomorrow.
You can always be sure that it lurks just ahead
  And in dreams find the cure for all sorrow.

You can measure success in terms of the present
  And live your life fully each day;
For success doesn't dwell in your memories or dreams
  But in steps that you take on the way.

NEW BEGINNINGS

Each chapter that is ending
    Leads us to a new beginning.
The past that we are leaving
    Means a future we are winning.

Each change that fills the present
    Sets the stage for our tomorrow,
And how we meet each challenge
    Helps determine joy or sorrow.

In every new beginning
    Spirit plays a vital part.
We must approach tomorrow
    With a strong and steady heart.

So as we turn the corner
    Let's all apprehension shed
And fill our hearts with confidence
    As we proceed ahead.

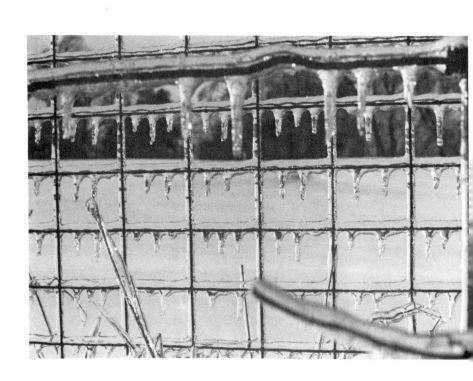

CREATIVITY IS...

Creativity is:

Finding space to play.

Playing until it becomes work.

And then working until it becomes play.

THE CREATIVE PERSON

You're the one who has the spark,
    Who keeps the ideas flowing,
Whose bright imagination
    Helps to keep the pace from slowing.

You're the one who has the gift,
    Who searches without ceasing,
Whose inspiration always
    Through hard effort is increasing.

You're the one who has the drive,
    Who struggles to uncover
All that acquiescent minds
    Aren't likely to discover.

You're the one who sorts the choices,
    Seeks the combinations,
And drawing from your boundless spirit
    Yields the innovations.

You're the one pursuing goals
    Your talents can immerse in.
In your unique, distinctive way,
    You're the creative person.

THE GIFT OF TEACHING

I've learned from you in many ways—
    You have the gift of teaching.
You've shared with me your knowledge,
    Always sensed when I was reaching.

I feel that you've enriched my life—
    You've influenced my thinking.
You've led me into learning,
    Kept my eagerness from shrinking.

You've broadened me with challenge,
    Entertained me with your style.
You've opened up my interest
    By eliciting a smile.

I've sensed the many moments
    When your wit and wisdom glistened.
I'll long recall the times
    When you have taught and I have listened.

IDENTITY PRAYER

Let me live and let me love
    And let me flourish free.
Let me be a total person—
    Let me know I'm me.

Let me grow and let me change
    To reach my true potential.
Let me choose important things,
    Reject the nonessential.

Let me listen, let me see
    The truths that others bring.
Let me savor human warmth—
    Let me laugh and sing.

Let me be secure enough
    To state my wants and needs.
Let me have enough to give
    Through words as well as deeds.

Let me find out who I am,
    Explore my definition.
Let me be in my own way
    A vital first edition!

BUMBLEBEE

Bumblebee in grasp of death,
    Bumblebee with talons tight,
Nursing nectar 'til the end
    Without the will to flee in flight.

Bumblebee in ecstasy
    As raucous rotors near,
Clinging to the very last
    Without a trace of fear.

Bumblebee embracing life,
    You have no need to fly;
Bumblebee, in pure devotion
    You will shortly die.

Bumblebee, at least you do not
    Fight the fates and fear them;
But rotors are the risks of life
    And I, alone, must hear them.

HOLY WAR

Anthill intervening
   In a quiet picnic outing:
Thrashing feet responding,
   Never second thoughts or doubting.

Lonely evening—sitting, watching,
   Spider crossing floor.
Couldn't hurt this living thing—
   That's what compassion's for.

What circumstance can separate
   The spider from the ant?
How can I spare the spider,
   Yet his plural cousin can't?

It seems that life is sacred
   On a lonely kitchen floor.
But when I am outnumbered,
   I declare a Holy War!

LUMINESCENCE

Flicker, flicker little life.
Lead me out of want and strife.
Guide me into love and hope.
Teach me how to care and cope.

Coddle me with faith and dreams.
Shelter me from coarse extremes.
Buoy me with eager breath.
Grant me life before my death.

NATURE'S FALL

The day had a perfect beginning,
  A crispness attached to the fall.
The mist and the leaves and the sunshine
  Were the sharpest this mind could recall.

The day was a tribute to autumn,
  To that cocktail of life known as air.
The sights and the sounds were staccato,
  A sensory symphony rare.

The nature that brought us this moment
  Is a nature ostensibly kind.
But life has its share of calamities
  That seize and take hold of the mind.

No earthquake or flood was the accent
  That caused my attention to bend.
It was a brief sight understated
  That brought this repose to an end.

My glance stumbled over a duo
  Of girls, about fourteen, I'd say.
The smoke wafting up from their cigarettes
  Blew sadness right into my day.

DON'T START

Here's a simple prescription
   To store in the heart:
You'll never get hooked
   If you'll just never start.

There are many temptations
   To darken your day.
There are many bad habits
   To lead you astray.

But the easiest answers
   Aren't always the best.
You're not always right
   When you follow the rest.

The quickest solutions,
   The pull of the crowd,
Can drag your bright future
   Right under a cloud.

No friend in his right mind
   Would ever deny it—
No lure can defeat you
   If you never try it.

The sadness that draws
   Friends and loved ones apart
Is surely avoided
   If you'll never start.

TO OUR HEALTH

As winds of fate and fortune change
And we assess our wealth,
Let's measure first what really counts—
The treasure of good health.

For there is no amount of money
We would take in trade
If merely for the sake of it
We let our good health fade.

Still, though we know the priceless nature
Of our own well-being,
We sometimes compromise our health
While fitness we're decreeing.

We borrow here and borrow there
With promise of repaying
And soon accumulate a debt
With interest quite dismaying.

So let's treat health from this day on
As if it's all we've got;
Let's not look back on squandered wealth
And say that we forgot.

PORTRAIT OF A GREEN THUMB

A green thumb knows the way to grow
  And how to keep things growing
And how to fertilize and weed
  And till the soil for sowing.

It takes a certain temperament
  To call the soil a friend,
To work with mother nature
  And her bounty to defend,

To revel in creation
  As the seasons ebb and flow
And continue planting indoors
  As the winter tempests blow.

It takes a love of living things
  And not just things material
To offer satisfaction
  So majestic and ethereal.

It takes a green thumb's patience
  To start with seedling small
And grow a thing of beauty
  Or a fruit so rich and tall.

When hard work brings the harvest
  And fulfills that basic yen,
It takes a true believer
  To start it all again.

DEWDROP

Life is like a flower;
    Hope is like a tear;
Love is like a dewdrop
    Awaiting to appear.

Morning is the sunlight,
    The mist a passing haze,
The dew a fragile meeting,
    A meshing with the days.

Night defines the daylight;
    It changes dew to tear;
It closes up the flower;
    It opens hope to fear.

But while the flower's open
    And dew adorns its petals,
Let's celebrate the flower
    Until the teardrop settles.

CLOSE TO LIFE

Today I'm close to life—
    I'm feeling comfortable with being.
The hours fill with light;
    The darker thoughts for now are fleeing.

I have a sense of fullness
    That the sun and air provide.
No pangs of insecurity
    Are nagging me inside.

I feast with this illusion;
    Then I sip its wine so rare.
I'm careful to remind myself
    These fruits aren't always there.

Some days I feel no fullness—
    I'm not comfortable at all.
I shed a tear as I observe
    How fast the shadows fall.

I then must seek out solace
    And subdue this inner strife;
I then must look around me
    To again be close to life.

YOUTH

Youth rides with us
  Until we're done.
It never notes
  The setting sun.

It only minds
  The way we see
A leaf upon
  November's tree.

If life is measured
  In the pall
Of this poor leaf
  About to fall,

Then youth and its
  Eternal dawn
Through this concern
  Is nearly gone.

But if that rusty
  Leaf we see
Still decorates
  This autumn tree,

Then youth stays with us
  'Til the end
Though wind and storm
  These branches bend.

CHALLENGER

I glide around my little pond
    Cutting meager wake,
Quite content to stay within
    The grasp of land and lake.

But there's another side of me
    Pursuing something more
That urges me to break the bonds
    Of earth and try to soar.

I must explore the limits
    That appear in wind and cloud.
I must assail the heavens,
    Seek out meanings soft and loud.

I have to struggle upward
    Into currents that are pure.
I have to sample freedom
    Before I am secure.

WHEN TIME STANDS STILL

The crystalline perfection
    Of a moment locked in time
Distills its true reflection
    Into memory sublime.

A day when progress halted
    And time, it seemed, stood still,
We sipped of pure simplicity
    And couldn't get our fill.

We focused on the plainer truths;
    We saw with clearer eyes;
We shunned the clutter in our lives
    And thus became more wise.

Life has certain jewels
    That are timeless and are rare.
They captivate us humbly
    In a breath of pure spring air.

A SPACE IN TIME

A crack in true eternal time
   Gives window to existence.
Mortal eyes so poignantly
   Record this precious distance.

Our brief moment lets us love
   This fragile gift of chance,
Filling eyes abundantly
   With life's resplendent glance.

Light my vision with awareness
   Of each fleeting second.
Let my senses shower
   In the warmth of hearts that beckoned.

Let us fill this crack in time
   And occupy our space
In such a way that time will say—
   Now, endlessly embrace.

TEARS OF SPRING

Hear my cry of Easter;
   See my tears of spring.
Find my fervent sun-filled hope
   Flying on the wing.

Fill my breath eternal.
   Warm my ageless love.
Firm my grasp on life itself.
   Gaze with me above.

Touch with me the fertile earth.
   Share my loving toil.
Find with me the laws of life.
   Liberate the soil.

Let me feel the sun and wind,
   Ingest the day and dawn.
Let me be a part of life
   Before this day is gone.

TAKE A MINUTE

Take a minute to reflect
    Upon the day just passed.
Take a minute to collect
    Sensations that will last.

Take a minute to enjoy
    The precious here and now.
Take a minute to explore
    The reasons why and how.

Take a minute to define
    The subtleties of love.
Take a minute to observe
    The mysteries above.

Take a minute to extract
    Some meaning from each other.
Take a special minute,
    Then another and another.

SURVIVOR

You lost your life in Vietnam;
  Your heart, it just gave out.
Your mind and spirit couldn't win—
  You lost the final bout.

They gave you up for gone
  But somehow found you in this war.
You came back home from Vietnam
  Much different than before.

You see, this blow to humankind
  Was much, much worse for you.
Your body had returned, but both
  Your heart and mind were through.

So many fell behind
  And lost it all on distant loam.
What hell it was to give your life,
  Then bring it with you home.

MIND AND SPIRIT

Life is a creative tablet,
　　A page to be written or drawn.
Life is a mode of expression,
　　A feeling that's captured or gone.

Life is a chain of emotions,
　　Of impulses straight from the heart.
Life is a song yet unwritten,
　　A voice still in search of a part.

Life is a vein of discovery,
　　A mine of incredible worth.
Life is a bright innovation
　　Ever awaiting its birth.

Life is a force that is forming,
　　A geyser about to erupt.
Life is a loud exclamation,
　　A message of meaning abrupt.

Life is a subtle revealing,
　　A poem about to emerge.
Life is the mind and the spirit
　　Finding the place to converge.

I'M ALONE WITH MYSELF

I'm alone with myself
  In the shelter of mind.
A certain companionship
  I seem to find:

A patience to hear
  And indulge all my fears;
A forum for freeing
  Invisible tears;

A listener hearing
  My wildest schemes;
A scriptwriter dealing
  In passionate themes;

A vent for my anger;
  A check on my pride;
A second opinion;
  A temperate guide;

A true confidant;
  A force catalytic;
A sometime supporter;
  A most frequent critic.

MELANCHOLY MOMENTS

There are melancholy moments
    When the world seems clear and pure.
Why these quiet moments
    Leave me thinking, I'm not sure.

There seems a fragile beauty
    So pervasive all around.
I'm always touched and grateful
    When this beauty can be found.

The seasons bring us to and from
    The fullness of creation;
And each approach and passing
    Brings us sadness, celebration.

For as we sense the rhythm
    Of sweet life and then of death,
We measure falling grains of sand
    And contemplate each breath.

SOJOURN WITH SLEEP

I slip into sleep;
    Soon I'm browsing with breath
Into caverns of consciousness
    Likening death.

I'm out of control—
    My deliberate mind
Is drifting, not knowing
    What echoes I'll find.

I like what I see,
    So enchanted by peace;
Will this calm overtake me
    When all functions cease?

Or will gentle slipping
    Seduce not at all
And the loss of the present
    Resemble a fall?

THE SEASON OF OUR SORROW

The loss of someone very dear
    Brings tears to those of us so near.
It drains the heart with untold sorrow,
    Leaves emptiness in our tomorrow.

All life, we know, must have its seasons;
    Yet death gives us no earthly reasons.
But just as winter finds relief
    In spring's rebirth, we know that grief

And all its future echoes bring
    A flood of memories just like spring.
A life so full is never gone
    As thoughts continue on and on.

A spirit so profusely shared
    Remains a gift to those who cared.
And memories of bright seasons past
    Mean that no season is the last.

MOTHER ROSE

Mother rose,
    With petals dear,
Your lifelong fragrance
    I will wear.

Your crystal freshness
    Lingers on.
Your reddest hue
    Is never gone.

From bud to bloom
    Your form has changed.
Your blossom's now
    From stem estranged.

Yet withered form
    With spirit free
Reminds me of
    What used to be.

And potpourri
    Of petals dear
Attracts, like dew,
    My treasured tear.

REMEMBER WITH THE HEART

Remember with the heart
   That bit of yesterday we shared.
Remember life as it was lived;
   Look back at how we cared.

Dwell upon the moments
   When our paths forever crossed.
Think about the love we gave,
   The part of us we lost.

Isolate the memory
   Of others we have known.
Liberate the love we felt,
   The warmth that we have shown.

Tell the mind to keep alive
   The spirit of the past.
Tell the heart to never part
   With special thoughts that last.

LITTLE BIRD

Little birdie you have fallen
   From your lofty nest.
We now must say goodbye
   And place you to eternal rest.

With leaves and dried up blades of grass
   As cushion for your head,
We place you with a gentle hand
   Atop your earthen bed.

I'm sad you never had a chance
   To stretch your wings and fly.
Your spirit strong was not enough
   To lift you to the sky.

But as you soar to greater heights
   While heeding nature's call,
I feel secure in knowing that
   You never more will fall.

MY PRAYER

Please listen to me
   As I pray.
I thank you, Lord,
   For this bright day.

I've noticed many
   Wondrous things—
The smallest plant,
   The bird that sings.

Tomorrow I shall
   Find still more.
Your precious gifts
   I won't ignore.

I'll cherish life
   In every form,
Find mystery
   In sun and storm.

I'll treat all others
   With respect.
My gift of life
   I won't neglect.

I'll live my life
   The best I can.
I'll guard your gifts
   Of love,
         Amen.

THE WINDOW

When my thoughts are probing deeper
   And my senses seem alone,
I see a shaded window
   Leading through to the unknown.

Its darkened front is always there—
    It masks the other side.
We never see behind to where
    Eternal secrets hide.

Then, ever so infrequently,
    This window turns to womb;
And, slipping through its portal,
    Someone leaves our lighted room.

The birth is such a puzzling one,
    A start that is an end;
It's hard when life abandons one
    Who labeled life as friend.

Such endings never let us
    Our perplexities forsake.
No glance comes back through windows
    When the glass is still opaque.

The heart that still is beating
    Cannot penetrate the view;
The heartbeat that is lost to time
    Can't send a message through.

But all that blocks our vision
    Fills the eyes with certainty
That through life's darkened window
    We eventually will see.

HOME IS IN THE HEART

When asked where does the home reside,
    I fondly said, "Inside, inside."
When thoughts of places I had lived
    Welled up within, I softly cried.

When asked where do these feelings start,
    I then replied, "The heart, the heart."
I know their penetrating force
    When finally I must depart.

In spaces where my memories roam
    I conjure up the home, the home—
That state of mind which rests upon
    A special portion of the loam.

What consecrates a dwelling so
    As hallowed place?—I know, I know.
It's where we exercise our dreams
    And find that needed space to grow.

As we along life's highways ride,
    While bounties of the earth provide,
We find that special place, the home,
    Which beckons us inside, inside.

TOM

Tom, our collie labrador,
　　Was often one to roam;
But when he did, we always knew
　　That Tom was coming home.

He savored wide expanses
　　And he often traveled far.
He followed old abandoned roads,
　　Devoid of truck or car.

And when he reached his destination,
　　Guided by his senses,
He then turned back along those roads
　　Where stones were piled as fences.

Though relishing the outdoor life
　　With all its furry creatures,
He readily returned to home
　　With its familiar features.

Panting hard at journey's end,
　　He had a certain glow.
He settled down to free himself
　　Of burs or icy snow.

He had his place amidst us all,
    Reclining ever near.
While chasing rabbits in his sleep,
    He had a listening ear.

He followed us for many years,
    A shadow unrelenting.
He lived his life and joined in ours,
    So eagerly assenting.

He slept right there beside our beds;
    He nudged us for attention.
He sensed our every change in mood,
    Divining each intention.

He licked the children in the face,
    His gentleness prevailing.
He was our true protector,
    Even with his senses failing.

He weathered imperceptibly,
    With gray around his muzzle.
A little lame, he traveled less,
    Not questioning life's puzzle.

We shared his love and gave him ours,
  Through youth and later years.
But then one day he left us all—
  He left us all in tears.

We wouldn't hear his bark again
  Nor feel his cold wet nose.
We wouldn't sense his warming presence
  Down around our toes.

Intent on new discovery,
  He exited our world.
He wagged his tail before his loving
  Spirit was unfurled.

And though we knew how much
  Our dear old dog preferred to roam,
We always knew that in the end
  Our Tom was coming home.

A BABY'S SMILE

Among our treasured thoughts we file
    The image of a baby's smile,
For there is something we all know
    Recaptured in that infant glow.

It speaks of language just unfolding
    And young impressions newly molding,
With logic so profoundly simple
    That all is said with laugh and dimple.

It speaks of motives plain and clear
    Expressed with glee or flood of tear
And tells of worries not yet forming
    And adult cares before their storming.

No self-awareness mars this smile,
    So innocent a baby's style;
It lets us know that all humanity
    Had at first no trace of vanity.

It says to us a babe is trusting
    Before the years of long adjusting.
With look of infant purity,
    It radiates security.

But the thing that makes this smile outrageous
    Is that it tends to be contagious.

Despite our own predisposition
    We match this smile of recognition
And find our simple interaction
    The cause of boundless satisfaction.

In drawing on an inner source,
    We tap a smile of youthful force;
And out of mutual elation
    We two become one generation.

A CHILD'S WORLD

The world's a place of warmth and joy
    For cherished infant girl or boy,
A place where he or she first smiled
    And life seemed large in the eyes of a child.

The world's a place for babes to crawl,
    For walking, too, and standing tall,
For running fast, with mishaps mild,
    And looking out through the eyes of a child.

The world's a place so near to home
    From whose wide bounds you seldom roam,
A place where blocks and toys are piled
    And life is rich in the eyes of a child.

The world's a place of neighbors' yards,
    Of fluffy dolls and baseball cards,
Of playgrounds where the hours are whiled
    And friends are formed in the eyes of a child.

The world's a place of schools and learning
    And seeing how the world is turning,
Of facts and figures quick compiled
    And wisdom gained through the eyes of a child.

The world's a place for puppy love
    And dreaming of the stars above
And styles parents think are wild
    And seeing change through the eyes of a child.

The world's a place for longer strides,
    For sensing life's divergent tides,
For charting out a course self-styled
    And seeing less through the eyes of a child.

The world's a place where life matures,
    Where in the heart our youth endures,
Where fondest memories long are filed
    Of how life looks through the eyes of a child.

Our hard and fast friend, *Mortimer Speed*.

TODAY'S CHILD

Look at a child, then look at the sky
  With its stars and its planets unchanging;
Then gaze at the child, so poised and so ready
  To rocket through stages far ranging.

Look at a child, then look at the sky—
  In the breath of a meteor's flight
A little one's grown and quickly flown
  Through childhood moments bright.

Look at a child, then look at the sky
  Where stars for eons last;
Then savor childhood's fleeting joys
  Before their glow is past.

A SISTER IS FOREVER

A sister's a sister forever,
   A bond that diminishes never,
A friend who is kindly and caring,
   A sibling God chooses for sharing.

Few ties are as deep and profound
   And with so much affection abound.
Though some thoughts are seldom expressed,
   Love endures and survives every test.

Of the constants that rest in the heart,
   A sister's a primary part.
She'll always be there when you need her—
   You listen, you value, you heed her.

As growth, independence you ponder,
   Your feelings grow deeper and fonder;
And life tells you one thing that's true:
   A sister's a large part of you.

LITTLE GIRL

Little girl with golden curl
    And words of pure invention,
Share with me your precious world—
    Immerse me with attention.

Bother me with wonder;
    Encumber me with awe;
Tickle me with nonsense
    In everything you draw.

Distract me with your interest
    In everything I do.
Pour out your emotions
    When your little heart is blue.

Tease me with your fantasies;
    Let bright impressions shine.
Bathe me with your knowledge;
    And deliver me from mine.

Carry me as passenger
    In a wagon made for two.
Remind me we will always be
    Just children passing through.

My heartfelt thanks to the following:

A caring family that left nothing unverbalized.

An eighth grade teacher who drummed the laws of grammar into my head while imploring me to discover and use my creative abilities.

My University of Rochester professor whose poetic archetypes became my elusive goal.

The U.S. Army's sleep-inducing curriculum which jump-started my creative energies and made me look at life through verse.

An editor of a national newspaper who posed as a conservative but, with true liberal spirit, gave my light verse a byline on his back page.

My parents who gave me the example of creativity by their every action and who believed in me as I searched for my own course in life.

My wife, Sydney, whose eighteen years of dedication taught me to tolerate myself and to love another.

My two children who taught me about "wondrous things."

Forty-two years of life which branded me with compassion, humor and occasional intolerance.